SARAH BERNHARDT IN THE
THEATRE OF FILMS AND
SOUND RECORDINGS

SARAH BERNHARDT IN THE THEATRE OF FILMS AND SOUND RECORDINGS

David W. Menefee

Foreword by Kevin Brownlow

McFarland & Company, Inc., Publishers
Jefferson, North Carolina, and London

Frontispiece: Sarah Bernhardt in the title role of
Phèdre (Racine), ca. 1874.

LIBRARY OF CONGRESS CATALOGUING-IN-PUBLICATION DATA

Menefee, David W., 1954–
Sarah Bernhardt in the theatre of films
and sound recordings / David W. Menefee ;
foreword by Kevin Brownlow.
p.   cm.
Includes bibliographical references and index.

ISBN 0-7864-1636-X (illustrated case binding : 50# alkaline paper) ∞

Bernhardt, Sarah, 1844–1923.   2. Actors — France — Biography.
3. Bernhardt, Sarah, 1844–1923 — Discography.
4. Berhnardt, Sarah, 1844–1923 — Career in motion pictures.   I. Title.
PN2638.B5M46   2003   792.02'8'092 — dc22   2003017741

British Library cataloguing data are available

Front cover: Sarah Bernhardt pictured in a one-sheet
advertising poster, circa 1919 *(Collection of Peter van der Waal)*;
Back cover: Sarah Bernhardt in a 1912 studio portrait from
Queen Elizabeth; *Background ©2003 PhotoDisc*

Manufactured in the United States of America

*McFarland & Company, Inc., Publishers
Box 611, Jefferson, North Carolina 28640
www.mcfarlandpub.com*

Acknowledgments

I am grateful to my mother and father, Eunice and Doyle Menefee, who told me there was a purpose to my life.

I am thankful for Sheila Soman, who shared with me her love for the unique voice of Sarah Bernhardt, relentlessly hunted down her recordings, and painstakingly translated many of them.

My gratitude is huge to Peter van der Waal who encouraged me to write this book and donated many photos from his personal collection.

I appreciate R. J. Maturi, who shared valuable material from his tireless research.

I was frequently helped by Ailene Bodholdt, who stopped whatever she was doing each time I needed help with a digital photo and solved my problems, even if it meant staying past quitting time.

Diane Paradiso from WPA Film Library was a wonderful contributor of still photos extracted from their archive collection.

Kate Stanworth from the British Film Institute earns my applause for helping to research many rare photos.

I could not have procured the frame enlargements from the *Duel d'Hamlet* film without the kind help of my friend Michael Derfler.

Rosemarie van der Zee and the Filmmuseum Berlin-Stiftung Deutsche Kinemathek kindly donated frame enlargements from their archive copy of *Duel d'Hamlet*.

Kristine Krueger from the Margaret Herrick Library of the Academy of Motion Picture Arts and Sciences Center for Motion Picture Study and National Film Information Service boosted this manuscript with many rare articles she researched from their vast files.

I am in debt to Randy Jones, who enabled me to create all the digital files of the manuscript and photos by volunteering to spend an entire weekend setting up a computer system.

Ronald Raburn was the greatest of help with the photo restorations, training me in the subtle nuances of digital enhancement techniques and sharing with me the mysterious secret of the gaussian blur.

Janet Perryman generously tutored me in the artistic design of illustrations, sharing her talent, and guiding me through the tedious techniques of photo layering.

A special thank you to Kurt Nauck of Nauck's Vintage Records for donating valuable images of Sarah Bernhardt's recordings.

Alain Campignon, from the family of Sarah Bernhardt, generously contributed a photo from his family album, of his Great-Grandfather, Maurice Bernhardt.

Professor Alissa Webel who spent many hours translating Sarah Bernhardt recordings.

Contents

Acknowledgments   v
Foreword by Kevin Brownlow   1
Preface   3
General Introduction   7

PART 1: BIOGRAPHY OF SARAH BERNHARDT

Early Years: From Student to Star   13
Touring the World   18
Lou-Tellegen   28
Quand Même   35

PART 2: SOUND RECORDINGS

Introduction   41
Audiography   47
1902 — *La Fiancée du Timbalier*   50
1902 — *Lucie*   51
1903 — *Le Lac (The Lake)*   52
1903 — *La Samaritaine*   54
1903 — *Les Vieux (The Old Ones)*   56
1903 — *Un Evangel (A Gospel)*   58
1903 — *Phèdre*   60
1903 — *La Mort d'Izail (The Death of Izail)*   62
1903 — *Théroigne de Méricourt's Dream (Le Rêve de Théroigne de Méricourt)*   63
1903 — *Un Peu de Musique*   66
1908 — *Les Bouffons: La Brise Conte (The Breeze Tells)*   67
1910 — *L'Aiglon: Act V, Scene V*   71
1910 — *Phèdre: Act II, Scene V*   75
1910 — *La Samaritaine: Act I, Scene V*   79

1918—*L'Etoile dans la Nuit* (*The Star in the Night*)   83
1918—*Prière pour Nos Ennemis* (*A Prayer for Our Enemies*)   84

PART 3: FILMS

Introduction   89
1900—*Le Duel d'Hamlet*   96
1908—*La Tosca*   97
1911—*La Dame aux Camélias*   100
1912—*Sarah Bernhardt à Belle Isle*   107
1912—*Les Amours de la Reine Elisabeth*   109
1913—*Adrienne Lecouvreur*   117
1915—*Ceux de Chez Nous*   119
1915—*Jeanne Doré*   121
1917—*Mères Françaises*   130
1919—*It Happened in Paris*   138
1921—*Daniel*   140
1923—*La Voyante*   146

Author's Note   151
Appendix: Chronological Listing of Plays, Films, and Recordings Performed by Sarah Bernhardt   152
Bibliography   155
Index   157

Foreword

by Kevin Brownlow

Sarah Bernhardt is a precious icon for film enthusiasts, for she represents the arrival of the feature film. Her *Queen Elizabeth* was shot almost a century ago yet it is still in circulation. It portrays a theatrical performance. As such it is of enormous historical importance, but as a fledgling feature it is basic. In no way does it suggest the incredible technical advances that would occur in the next fifteen years before the arrival of sound put it all back to square one, and pictures were photographed for a while in exactly the same way.

You could not guess from *Queen Elizabeth* what a mesmerizing stage actress Bernhardt was or what a tempestuous character. I met some of those who worked with her and some, like John Gielgud, who saw her on stage and never forgot the experience. "It was during the First World War," said Gielgud. "She was in a playlet, *Au Champ d'Honneur*, at the Coliseum where she used to come and play often. She'd already lost her leg and was lying on the stage under a rug dressed as a Poilu with beautiful makeup and a boy's wig. A Red Cross officer came up to tend to her and she found a standard in a tree behind where she was lying and she clutched it to her bosom and then she rose to a sitting position and leveled a great aria of patriotism and fell back dead at the end

of it. Then I remember the call — she was standing with her hand on the shoulder of the man who played the doctor, so she could take her call. I was very impressed by that, and the voice sounded marvelous. I was sitting as a schoolboy fourteen rows back so she looked perfectly young to me, but I suppose she was tremendously made up. Then I saw her in clips from *Queen Elizabeth* and *La Dame aux Camélias*, in all of which I thought she looked grotesque and never stopped waving her arms about and obviously speaking the lines of the play, which didn't work."

The extracts Gielgud saw were certain to have been crude dupes, shown at the wrong speed. David Menefee has tracked the best surviving copies to the archives that preserve them and issues an appeal for them to be released from their imprisonment. This requires money, but as so vital a part of the heritage of France, the French cultural ministry should make it a priority to have these transferred to DVD in the same way as the Lumière films were given to the public for the cinema's centenary. As a tribute to French culture, what could be more relevant?

For the films are all we have as a visual record of a great artist, and if shown in good prints at the right speed, they will provide a fresh image of Bernhardt. Thanks to David

1

Menefee, we can see these performances through his eyes and can realize the riches in store for us.

We film historians are familiar with *Queen Elizabeth*. What is so surprising about this book is its revelations of other films made by Bernhardt, including one made in Hollywood and one shot during World War I within the range of the German guns. Bernhardt began by despising the cinema. This was ironical, because by appearing on the screen she did more than anyone to dignify it.

Forty years ago, I had a meeting with a man who played a significant role in the Bernhardt saga. In December 1964, I entered the Paramount building at 1501 Broadway and was sent up by elevator to the ninth floor. Here a secretary ushered me into the presence of the founding father of the feature film, Adolph Zukor. It was a bit like meeting Miss Havisham from *Great Expectations*. He was very small and very old — practically ninety-two — and he worked in what must have been his original office. It was oak paneled, with faded photographs on the wall of personalities such as Jesse Lasky, Zukor's partner. A sepia-toned Victorian photo of Mrs. Zukor was on his desk. A clock chimed gently in the background. Once we got going he gave no impression of age — although at one point he said, "I can't do today what I could do thirty or forty years ago by any means."

An immigrant from Hungary, who had arrived in New York seventy-six years before I met him, he had started in the fur business and had become involved with movies through the Hales Tours, a device which gave the impression of rail travel. He felt the only way to improve the motion picture business and to make it respectable was to introduce films of the same length as plays, with the same stars as the stage. With enormous chutzpah, he aimed at the Star.

"I had financed a picture, *Queen Elizabeth*, which was made in Paris in 1912. I had obtained the American rights for that picture. All other rights belonged to a fellow named J. Frank Brockliss. Mercanton (he pronounced it Mark Anton, like a character from *Julius Caesar*) was the director of the picture. The plan was all worked out in England, and they had approached Sarah Bernhardt before her season closed in the spring of 1911. It required quite a bit of convincing Sarah Bernhardt that this was something that would remain in existence for posterity. So if you want to perpetuate yourself for future generations, in addition to the compensation, I told her, you will have great satisfaction. So while she could always use money, she wasn't anxious enough to take money if she felt it would bring her down instead of lifting her up. And I paid her. The amount that she received was $40,000 in American money. That was an awful lot of money in those days, even in America, for a motion picture. After the launch of that picture was successful, we decided to form the Famous Players Company and use famous names and famous personalities in established plays and produce them for the screen."

This was the start of what became the multimillion dollar Paramount Corporation. Zukor told me that Paramount has just made a new negative of *Queen Elizabeth*.

David Menefee also includes a detailed history of Bernhardt's recordings. I have never heard that celebrated "honey voice," and I suspect they will conjure up the personality even more strongly than the films. Taken together, the career recorded in this book — in its silent and sound aspects — would be enough for any ordinary mortal. But all this was in addition to what was perhaps the best-remembered stage career in history. Sarah Bernhardt was a phenomenon.

Preface

"Sarah Bernhardt made movies? The only one I ever heard of was *Queen Elizabeth*." This comment is typical of the response made when the subject of Sarah Bernhardt films and sound recordings is broached. *Queen Elizabeth* has been written about extensively in nearly every book about motion picture history because it galvanized the progress of early cinema, pushing the format from one-reel films into the dimension of feature-length productions. Prints of the film have been in circulation continually since the 1912 production in every known film format. The Museum of Modern Art in New York occasionally screens their 35mm print to packed theaters of curious patrons who still come to see the legend come to life once again.

In the film *The Seven-Year Itch*, Marilyn Monroe, playing an aspiring actress in television commercials, turns to Tom Ewell and says, "I wish I had been old enough to have seen Sarah Bernhardt. Was she great?" I wondered about this, also.

I was a young theater student in the 1960s at Rosemont Junior High School in Fort Worth, Texas. While sitting in the library one day, my gaze wandered to a small book on the bottom shelf with the title *Great Lady of the Theater*. I took the book home and while reading the manuscript discovered the legend of Sarah Bernhardt for the first time. To my surprise, Sarah Bern-

hardt was lifted up on a pedestal as the pinnacle of achievement in theater, a lofty position that was said to be greater than that of any other actor. I wanted to know more about her, and my curiosity was greatly enriched when another book was released in 1966, Cornelia Otis Skinner's *Madame Sarah*. I was thrilled by a few sentences that claimed this great star had made some films. These few, brief mentions were all that was said about those films, as if they were of no importance. Seeing Sarah in films, I imagined, would be the next best experience to seeing her perform live. From that time I became obsessed with finding those films and experiencing the legend for myself.

As fate would have it, I discovered an 8mm-film distributor who was circulating a copy of *Queen Elizabeth*, Sarah's 1912 epoch-making production. I worked one entire summer at a youth camp to earn the thirty-five dollars required to purchase a print. With a borrowed projector from my grandmother Elsie Menefee, I had my first experience of witnessing a performance of Sarah Bernhardt. She was everything I had expected, and her style, grace, power and temperament were all gloriously displayed in this film. But I was still unsatisfied, having had a taste, and I wanted to see more of her work.

While combing the library in downtown Fort Worth, I learned that Sarah had

An early publicity photograph compositing various stage roles of Sarah Bernhardt. It appeared on a poster used as part of the marketing for Sarah Bernhardt's appearance in vaudeville ca. 1912.

made other films, and as if this weren't enough to whet my appetite, I discovered she had also made sound recordings of her plays. When I heard one for the first time, my mind was blown away by the incredible sound of her voice. The unique vibrato, the dramatic power of her delivery and emotional displays were unlike any performance I had heard before.

I began to research everything I could find all over the world about this artist. As time went by, the snippets of information began to grow into quite a stack of papers. I finally decided to compile this research into a cohesive, chronological whole. My path had led me into contact with many other people who were also enraptured with Sarah. It became important to give these fans a manuscript that explored her work in films and sound recordings. She was the supreme master of vocal technique and stagecraft, the bar to which all aspiring actors must attempt to reach. Her existing performances deserve to be studied, explored and savored.

What you will find in this book is the first-ever, in-depth exploration of Sarah Bernhardt's films and sound recordings. Sheila Soman and Professor Alisa Webel have painstakingly transcribed and translated her recordings into French and English for review for the first time.

Her unknown, lost film of *Daniel*, made in 1921, was discovered hidden in a film vault in the United States. This film is explored here for the first time, in addition to all of her other films.

Sarah Bernhardt pictured in a one-sheet advertising poster circulated in many stage and motion picure theaters around 1919 (from the collection of Peter van der Waal).

My greatest hope is that Sarah's fans and those curious about her work will find their interest piqued by the revelations in this book and that somehow those distant archives that hide her films in the darkness of cold, isolated vaults will bring them back to the piercing light of modern projectors.

"There are five kinds of actresses," said Mark Twain, "bad actresses, fair actresses, good actresses, great actresses and Sarah Bernhardt."

General Introduction

Sarah Bernhardt was a living legend and a theatrical superstar of the nineteenth century, the same as Mary Pickford, Charlie Chaplin, Rudolph Valentino, Frank Sinatra, Elvis Presley and the Beatles were in the twentieth century. Unlike these later artists, Sarah created her own fame initially without the use of television, recordings, or motion pictures. She had to rely solely on the publicity generated by continuous tours of her live theater performances. Sarah toured by train in both hemispheres of the world, taking her players with her, and had the additional burden of transporting the sets from place to place. The troupe performed endless repetitions of her popular plays to thrilled audiences.

Photography played a vital role in the publicity surrounding her productions. Postcards, cabinet cards, character portraits, cigarette cards, and posters were designed and widely circulated to fan the flame of her notoriety and to increase public awareness of her image. Sarah understood the power of the photograph, and many of the images that document her work retain the mesmerizing impact she is reputed to have had on live audiences.

The inventor Thomas Edison surprised the world with his incredible phonograph and W. K. L. Dickson's kinetoscope recording devices. Sarah was destined to cross Edison's path, and in 1880, while on an American tour, Sarah made her first audio recording at his home. In 1900 Sarah ventured into the medium of motion pictures for the first time. She was attracted to the idea of using moving pictures of her stage work as a valuable tool for publicity, as well as an opportunity to record her work for posterity. Always the adventurer, Sarah was one of the first stage stars to appear in the movies.

Charles Ford, in his essay titled "Notes on a Dying Legend" in *Films in Review* (1954), wrote, "It is often said that the great French tragédienne, Sarah Bernhardt, was indirectly responsible for the success of one of the most powerful of the American producing companies. And there are even some who give her exclusive credit for the tremendous development of the whole picture industry."

Not everyone agreed. The public liked the silent film version of *Queen Elizabeth* in which Sarah performed, but the critics did not. One reviewer wrote, "Sarah Bernhardt was more unacquainted with the supreme art of silence than anyone else, more than all the other actors of the speaking theater. For half a century she had known how to win glory by expressing the gamut of emotions with her golden voice. All of a sudden, an actress of genius, accustomed to expressing herself by giving words their maximum value, is asked to forgo her technique and express herself by gestures only. The result is lamentable."

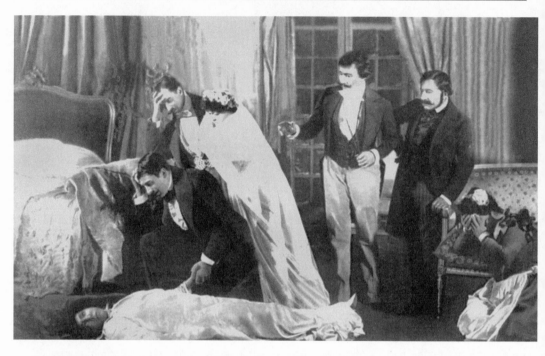

Sarah Bernhardt in the stage play of *La Dame aux Camélias* (1880), in the classic moment of her tragic demise.

"Although *Queen Elizabeth* had little enough to recommend it," wrote Charles Ford, "and deserves attention only because of its influence on the American motion picture industry, it provoked a veritable sensation when Adolph Zukor opened it at New York's Lyceum Theater in July of 1912. He had no trouble renting prints all over the United States and in a short time his company, 'Famous Players' had a net profit of $60,000 and was a viable business."

A year later, in the course of Bernhardt's tour of the United States, the film's success was so extreme that her male costar, Lou-Tellegen, left her to settle in Hollywood, embarking on a new career as a silent film matinee idol.

Of the great stage actresses who bequeathed their art to film posterity, certainly Sarah Bernhardt started earliest, lasted longest and had the greatest influence. Despite claims in various later biographies that she hated films and did them only for the money, Sarah seemed fascinated by the process of film making. In 1913 and 1915 she made extensive home movies of herself, family and friends and gave elaborate screenings to show them off. "It is the wonder of the age," she said of the movies in 1915. "I must confess that it was the novelty of the idea which first led me to act before the camera. But since then I have become greatly impressed with the utility of moving pictures, and although I have acted before the camera so little, I feel diffident about venturing an opinion."

Sarah found the experience of viewing her performances on film to be a rare opportunity for critical self-study. She observed that, "If I could have watched myself in motion pictures at rehearsals I would have been a better actress."

A year before her death Bernhardt published a novel titled *Jolie Susie*, in which one of the principal characters says, "I believe the movies could be the school of an easy culture and could popularize all the sciences and all forms of progress. But the directors of the film companies are like the Germans, who have used the finest inventions for crime and death."

Sarah loved the movies, and this fact is proven by the explicit testimony of Jacques Feyder. In 1920, when he produced *Atlantide*, he gave the male lead to Jean Angelo, a godson of Bernhardt's, and invited her to a private showing. "For three hours," he wrote, "the picture silently rolled on without musical accompaniment, without a word. The lights came on and the great Sarah, at the end of a life of unequalled glory, said to me after a sigh: "What a pity they did not invent the cinema sooner. What a career I could have had!"

W. G. Maxcy, in a speech to the Candlelight Club on Nov. 22, 1922, said, "The movies are the greatest blessing that ever came to mankind, both as entertainment and for education. They furnish the best amusement for all the people. There is no other amusement or recreation that reaches all the people in the world like the movies. The pleasure of the automobile can only be indulged in by those who can afford to support Rockefeller and the garage men. The opera can only be indulged in by the millionaire class. The best musical comedies and speaking plays can only be enjoyed by those who are what we call well-to-do or rich. Horse racing, yachting, and sports of that kind are only for the rich, but the movie is for everyone. Great or small, rich or poor, educated or illiterate, there is a movie for them all.

Sarah Bernhardt in 1909 as Le Poète and Mlle. Martet as La Muse in *La Nuit de Mai* (from the collection of Peter van der Waal).

"The children of the poor must have entertainment that enables them to let off steam just as well as the rich man's child. The poor boy cannot indulge in those luxury pastimes of the wealthy, so he goes to the movies. There he can see some man rescue the beautiful lady from the grasp of the bandit, just as the rich boy does when his team wins.

"When I think of the wonderful benefit that the moving picture has been to everyone during the trying times since the World War started in 1914, to lose themselves for a

To Sarah Bernhardt, author unknown. This poem, from a magazine published by Martin Beck in 1912 while Sarah was touring in vaudeville, celebrates her renown as the Lady of the Golden Voice.

ticket. The movies brought her art to the common man in a way that fifty years of touring live performances could not. People who had only heard of her from others could actually see her in the movies.

She completed twelve motion pictures, and only four of those were full-length dramas, the others playing for durations of one or two reels. Ten of the films are known to have survived the ravages of a passing century, two world wars and nitrate film decomposition.

Her sound recordings give us just a flavor of the power and beauty of her vocal delivery, her unique vibrato and powerful style. Fortunately, most of those recordings have survived.

The "divine Sarah" is something more than the finest of tragédiennes; she is a human monument to the art of acting, a connecting link with the heroic days of dramatic poetry, of Dumas, Sardou, and Victor Hugo. Her acting remains the standard of merit in fifty classic parts; she has illuminated the great works of the greatest Frenchmen, from Racine to Rostand, from Sardou to Bisson. Not to have seen Sarah Bernhardt is to have missed the most important chapter in the histrionic history of our age.

Fortunately, her art was preserved in motion pictures and sound recordings. This book is an exploration of those films and recordings of Sarah Bernhardt's fragile attempt to earn immortality.

short time in the pleasures derived from looking at the pictures on the screen, it seems as though it was a part of the plan of the great power that is ruling this universe to give us in this time of need this cheap and easily obtained recreation and relaxation from our worries, our troubles and our trials, and I feel like thanking God for the movies."

Sarah's plays were given to the masses all over the world but only to those fortunate enough to afford the high price of a

"I depend on these films for my immortality."
— Sarah Bernhardt

Part 1

BIOGRAPHY OF
SARAH BERNHARDT

Early Years: From Student to Star

Sarah Bernhardt (1844–1923), a French actress, was one of the great international stage stars of her time. She was celebrated for her graceful movements, the hypnotic spell she held over audiences and the bell-like clarity of the unique vibrato of her voice. She also won praise for the heightened emotional and physical realism of her acting.

She was born in Paris. Her real name was Henriette-Rosine Bernard. She was the daughter of a beautiful woman who earned her living entertaining wealthy gentlemen. Her early years were spent in a fairly normal childhood, much of which was at a convent. On the eve of her fifteenth birthday a family council assembled, and her fate was settled for all time. Her mother; her aunt, Rosine; Mlle. de Brabender, her governess; a notary from Le Havre; her godfather; her uncle M. Meydieu; and the Duc de Morny, a family friend, met at their home to hold court on her behalf to decide what was to be done about her future.

In her autobiography, *My Double Life: The Memoirs of Sarah Bernhardt* (translated by Victoria Tietze Larson), Sarah wrote about this wrenching meeting between herself and her well-intentioned family:

"Well, as we have come here on account of this child," said her godfather, "we must begin and discuss what is to be done with her." Her mother spoke very slowly. "At times it seems to me that she is quite idiotic. She quite disheartens me," she revealed to the gathering. "It appears you want to be a nun," said M. Meydieu. "You have to be rich, though, to enter a convent, and you have not a sou."

"I have the money that Papa left," Sarah whispered.

"Your father left some money to get you married," said the notary.

"Well then, I'll marry God," Sarah answered as she slipped away from the group. "I will be a nun, I will!"

After this explosive tirade, giving every reason why she wanted to be a nun, some members of the group were speechless at her burst of confidence and determination. A few of them were impressed at her histrionic display of emotion.

"Do you know what you ought to do with this child?" asked the Duc de Morny. "You ought to send her to the Conservatoire."

The Conservatoire was the most

Sarah and her mother, Judith Van Hard, a beautiful and successful conqueror of men.

the Comédie Française, the leading theater in Paris, to see her first play. "When the curtain slowly rose, I thought I should have fainted. It was as though the curtain of my future life was being raised. That night the actors were performing in *Britannicus*. I heard nothing of *Britannicus* for I was far, far away," said Sarah. She was so moved by the performance that she burst into loud sobs, so loud that the whole house, very amused by her fit, looked up at the box in which she sat. Her mother was deeply annoyed and took her out. Her godfather was furious and muttered, "She ought to be shut up in a convent and left there! Good heavens, what a little idiot the child is!"

Soon after this eventful night, Sarah received a letter from her aunt telling her that M. Auber, who was then director of the Conservatoire, was expecting her the next day at nine in the morning to audition. In preparation for the examination, she was quickly rehearsed in a piece to present for the audition. On the day of the audition, Sarah was informed that she had to have another person with her to read her cues. Since she had failed to bring anyone to fill this role, it was impossible to perform the piece she had rehearsed. With a sudden decision, Sarah declared that she would recite a fable, "The Two Pigeons." Finally her name was called, and Sarah stood before a large table around which sat a group of men and one woman. The woman looked at her through an eyeglass and said, "Make your bow and commence, and then stop when the chairman rings." Sarah at once made a bow and began her recitation

prestigious school for beginning students of the theater.

"She is too thin to make an actress," one relative stated.

"I won't be an actress," Sarah screamed.

"You don't know what an actress is," said her aunt.

"Oh, yes I do. Rachel is an actress," answered Sarah.

"You know Rachel?" asked her mother, getting up from her chair.

"Oh, yes, she came to the convent once," was Sarah's emphatic reply.

"Send her to the Conservatoire," was the final opinion of all those present. To Sarah's ears the words were like a sentence to a fate worse than death.

That night Sarah's mother took her to

Left: Sarah in 1859, in a youthful portrait taken by Felix Nadar.

Right: Sarah Bernhardt in a youthful portrait by Felix Nadar.

of the tale of "The Two Pigeons." She was interrupted and criticized to speak louder. This confused and frightened her, and the table of judges laughed at her nervousness. When she recovered her will power and began the fable again, she was determined to overcome the shattering emotion of contempt she was feeling from the judges. Sarah later confessed, "My voice was more liquid from the emotion, and the desire to make myself heard caused it to be more resonant. The group around the table became silent, and before I had finished my fable, the little bell rang. I bowed and went down the few steps from the platform thoroughly exhausted."

She was accepted as a member of the Conservatoire. Soon after her studies began, Sarah won prizes for performances of both tragedy and comedy. She began fencing lessons and learned the art of the theater from the most distinguished teachers of the time.

She made her acting debut at the Comédie Française in 1862 in the title role of Jean Racine's classic tragedy *Iphigénie*. She was in five scenes of this production. The next day an article in *L'Opinion Nationale* reviewed her debut performance with these lines, "Mlle. Bernhardt, who made her debut yesterday in the role of Iphigenie, is a tall, pretty girl with a slender figure and a very pleasing expression. The

upper part of her face is remarkably beautiful. She holds herself well, and her enunciation is perfectly clear. This is all that can be said for her at present." Her debut had rated only a lukewarm comment.

A second appearance was on stage in a play called *Valérie*. This met with some slight success and was followed by a third appearance at the Comédie Française in *Les Femmes Savantes*. The reviews of her work in this play were not favorable.

Reviews during the next six months were even worse as she acted in half a dozen drab roles. The reporters ignored her presence in the casts until she found a way to break their lethal silence.

At a solemn performance in honor of Molière, Madame Nathalie, an overweight dowager veteran actress, tangled with Sarah in the foyer of the theater over an incident involving the train of her gown. Sarah's younger sister had accidentally stepped on the woman's train. The woman became irate and gave the child a shove, prompting Sarah to slap the actress. The woman then gave Sarah a shove. With shouts of "nasty beast," Sarah tore into her like a wild animal that resulted in the tribute to Molière being delayed until the swooning thespian could be carried out of the theater on a stretcher. The next day the managers of the theater charged Sarah with an official offense and ordered

Sarah Bernhardt as *Leah* (from the collection of Peter van der Waal).

Sarah Bernhardt as Zanetto, the strolling boy troubadour in Coppée's *Le Passant* (from the collection of Peter van der Waal).

her to apologize and pay a fine. Sarah refused.

Although she had been given a leading part in another play, she was removed from the cast and another actress was chosen. Her rejection was in the form of a letter from the directors of the theater. "I finished reading the letter through blinding tears, but very soon anger took the place of grief," Sarah recalled.

She tore up her contract with the Comédie Française, left the theater no longer a member, and did not return again for twelve years. Her tantrum cost her a job, but in the newspapers, the front-page treatment of her actions helped her land a better one. Sarah's godfather arranged for her to work at another theater called Théâtre du Gymnase. She understudied in one play

and performed in *La Maison sans Enfants*. While in these critical months of venue change Sarah became the mistress of Henri, Prince de Ligne, and gave birth to her only child Maurice.

She had great success in a piece called *Le Démon du Jeu*. There followed a series of plays at other theaters before Sarah landed a job at the Odéon and

Sarah Bernhardt portrait ca. 1877.

Sarah Bernhardt in her rosewood coffin, the famous, macabre photograph that shocked the world, a portrait taken while she was very much alive.

debuted in *Le Jeu de l'Amour et du Hasard*. Sarah was noted for her unusual voice and made a strong impression on the public in the role of Zacharie in a play called *Joad*. "Oh, that Odéon Theater," Sarah later said. "It is the theater I have loved most."

Convinced that a defamatory press pays off better at the box office than a silent one, Sarah kept the earthiest details of her life in newspaper and magazine headlines for the next half century. Her manner of dress, her off-stage preoccupations and her other artistic endeavors were reported as news. Bernhardt then took the attitude of a shy little violet whose shady dell has been desecrated. Editors received sharp letters from her demanding to be allowed a modicum of privacy. They frequently reproduced her letters on the pages of the following day's edition.

She quickly fashioned herself into a caricature with her frizzed hair frequently dyed to an ever-changing palate of colors. In an age when the "Gibson Girl" hourglass figure was the vogue, Sarah exaggerated her slimness by wearing long, clinging gowns of her own designs. Cartoonists were delighted to satirize her image with stinging caricatures. Jokes were circulated, such as "An empty carriage drove up, and out jumped Sarah Bernhardt."

It was at the Odéon that rehearsals begin for a play by François Coppée called *Le Passant*. It was a triumph. The opening night brought the whole house on their feet cheering over and over again. The curtain was raised eight times for Sarah. There followed more than a hundred consecutive performances at the Odéon, which played to full houses. Sarah found herself a star in a huge successful play for the first time. She became the queen of the students who came to the theater and was showered with flowers when arriving at the theater and cheered wildly by the students from the balconies during the play.

The Franco-Prussian war of 1870-1871, during which Paris was occupied, soon forced the closure of the theaters in Paris. Sarah's career went into suspension for many months while France was very nearly ruined by the devastation of battle.

After the war, the Odéon reopened its doors to the public, offering some new plays in which Sarah was again presented to the adoring public, who had not forgotten her. "I was, however, awaiting the event which was to consecrate me a star," Sarah said. "I did not quite know what I was expecting, but I knew that my messiah had to come. And it was the greatest poet of the last century who was to place on my head the crown of the elect." At the end of 1871 Victor Hugo asked Sarah to a reading of his play *Ruy Blas*.

The role of the queen was earmarked for Sarah. On the 26th of January, 1872, Sarah emerged brilliantly in this role. "I felt that I was destined for celebrity. Until that day I had remained the students' little fairy," Sarah claimed. "I became then the elect of the public." Her performance as the love-stricken queen was called "a thing of lyricism and beauty." The public fell totally under her spell, breathlessly in love with her, and they made *Ruy Blas* the hit of the season. It ran for many months, cementing Sarah as a notable image and voice in the minds of the public, a reputation that would remain to the present.

Touring the World

Sarah again was invited to join the famous Comédie Française with a contract and salary of 12,000 francs a year. On November 6, 1872, she opened in *Mademoiselle de Belle Isle* and made a complete failure of her debut. "My excuse, though, was not the stage fright to which Francisque Sarcey attributed it, but the terrible anxiety I felt on seeing my mother hurriedly leave her seat in the dress circle five minutes after my appearance on the stage," Sarah explained. "I uttered one word after another, stammering through my sentences haphazardly, with only one idea in my head, a longing to know what happened." Later Sarah heard her mother fled her seat because a lady seated near her said jeeringly, "Why, she's like a dried bone, this little Bernhardt!" When Sarah learned the reason for her mother's hasty exit from the theater, she was able to finish the play with confidence.

She continued her debut in *Junie de Britannicus*, *Le Mariage de Figaro*, *Dalila*, *L'Absent*, *Chez l'Avocat*, *Andromaque*, and *Phèdre*. But her frustration at not being allowed to play the parts she wanted gave way to anger and rebellion. She did not want to play in *Zaire* and determined to kill herself during the premier performance by giving everything she had of her heart and soul to the demands of the part, and, to vex her producers, to finish by dying on stage. To her surprise she found herself not only alive but also invigorated by the exertion. As Sarah pointed out, "Then I saw the possibility of the longed-for future. Not being able to die at will, I faced about and resolved to be strong, vivacious, and active, to the great annoyance of some of my contemporaries, who had put up with me only because they thought I would soon die, but

Sarah Bernhardt on tour aboard the *Sarah Bernhardt Special*. She loved to sit on the back porch as the train journed from state to state across America.

who began to hate me as soon as they acquired the conviction that I should perhaps live for a long time."

She became a great attraction, a huge box office draw, and filled the theater with more money than they had known before. Other notable roles during her second contract at the theater included the title character in Racine's *Phèdre*, *L'Etrangère*, *Rome Vaincu*, and *Hernani*.

In 1878 Sarah had felt the growing pains of her talent and, unable to vent her need for expression in the theater, tried her hand at sculpture, art and writing. Still unsatisfied, she began attempting daredevil stunts such as descending into an octopus garden in the sea and ascending into the clouds in a balloon called the "Doña Sol." The balloon had soared to nearly a mile and a half above the earth. "It was splendid! It was stupefying! The spectacle became fairy-like," she said. "Large fleecy clouds were spread below us. Large orange curtains fringed with violet came down from the sun to lose themselves in our cloudy carpet."

Her producers were not amused. Far below on the ground, the directors of the Comédie Française fumed at her capricious escapade. The following day they tore into her about her ill temper and eccentricities, fining her 40 francs for traveling without the consent of the manager. Sarah refused to pay the fine. She was sick of the pompous traditions of their theater and the limitations of the roles she was forced to play.

She continued to perform in the plays assigned to her, including a remake of *Ruy Blas*. This new version was as successful as the production at the Odéon. But her relations with the theater management continued to be strained. Her personal behavior greatly annoyed them. Sarah commented, "I had a continual thirst for what was new." There was also a continual cry of indignation against her. "This is how it is," she explained to the theater directors. "I have a wild desire to travel, to see something else, to breathe another air, and to see skies that are higher than ours and trees that are bigger. In short, something different." They were not enthusiastic about her desires.

Sarah sent her letter of resignation, but it was refused. "My fame had become annoying for my enemies, and a little trying, I confess, for my friends," Sarah revealed.

"But at this time all this stir and noise amused me vastly. I did nothing to attract attention, but my fantastic tastes, my paleness and thinness, my particular way of dressing, my scorn of fashion, my general freedom in all respects, made me a being set apart. I did not recognize this fact." She did realize that she was bringing in more money to the Comédie Française than anyone else and she might have enough influence to demand that her desires be satisfied. She also secretly thought about breaking away entirely.

An elderly Englishman called on her and offered the new opportunity she sought. "I am Mr. Jarrett, the impresario," he claimed. "I can make your fortune. Will you come to America?"

Sarah signed a contract with Mr. Jarrett to tour England and found in him a spirit for adventure matched only by her own desire for the new and unusual. Their association bonded, as she remembered in her autobiography, "with confidence at first sight, a confidence which he never betrayed." Their alliance quickly led to lucrative engagements playing in drawing rooms while the theater troupe was on a London tour. Her producers were again outraged at her exploitations and tried to force her to submit to their will.

The London tour was an enormous success, bolstering Sarah's taste for adventure and filling her purse with the kind of money her life demanded. Her successful work was making itself into a craze that grew beyond London. Her sculptures were selling at shows along the way. Offers were pouring in from all directions for appearances. She accepted many of them, much to the anger of the Comédie management. Their attitude only drove Sarah farther away from them until the constrictive engagement of the Comédie Française became more than she could bear. They asked her to appear in *L'Aventuriere*, a part she loathed. She forced herself to go through with the production,

Sarah Bernhardt as *Cléopâtre* (1890).

Sarah Bernhardt in a portrait taken in 1877.

and both she and the critics considered it to be the worst of her career.

Sarah again sent in her resignation and mailed copies to the local newspaper. Her decision was a final one.

Three days later Mr. Jarrett called again. For the third time he proposed to make a contract for an American tour. This time Sarah listened to his proposition, and she heard staggering figures: 5,000 francs for each performance and half the takings above 15,000 francs. In addition, 1,000 francs per week for her hotel, a special Pullman train car for the journey, a paid staff and two cooks. Sarah accepted everything as she was anxious to leave Paris. The road lay ahead, opening before her the entire world, and Sarah was elated to explore the new horizons across the Atlantic.

Above: Sarah Bernhardt as Marguerite Gautier in the stage play of *La Dame aux Camélias,* her most famous role (from the collection of Peter van der Waal). *Below:* Sarah Bernhardt assuming a prayerful pose in *La Dame aux Camélias.*

She planned a repertory of eight plays, *Froufrou, La Dame aux Camélias, Le Sphinx, Hernani, Phèdre, Adrienne Lecouvreur, L'Etranger* and *La Princesse George.* A quick tour of European cities tested the productions and perfected the presentations. After returning to Paris on September 30, 1880, she began final preparations for the tour of America. The press went wild over the prospect of her impending journey. Sarah wrote, "Up to the last moment, people in Paris did not believe that I would really go. I had such uncertain health that it seemed folly to undertake such a journey. But when it was quite certain that I was going, there was a general outburst from my enemies and the hue and cry after me was in full swing."

It was around this time that Sarah cre-

ated her signature role, *La Dame aux Camélias*, known in America as *Camille*. She played the dying courtesan more than 3,000 times in the theater, making the play her most dependable cash cow for decades. She had the foresight to identify her private life with the character in *Camille*, often securing lurid tabloid accounts of her alleged affairs. When tantrums failed to draw enough cash customers, rumors would leak out that she had taken a new lover, and Sarah supported these innuendos by surrounding herself with France's most eligible leading stars in the theater.

Despite the adverse criticism, Sarah embarked on a ship called *L'Amérique*, a boat haunted by accidents, storms at sea and fires. On the 15th of October, 1880, at six o'clock in the morning, Sarah set sail in a bewildering uproar of farewell kisses, sobbing, and goodbyes. For three days she stayed in her cabin and then emerged on a windy, gloomy day. There was a woman on board who spoke to nobody and was noted for her dismal expression and a demeanor of heavy mourning. One evening as Sarah passed the lady dressed in black, her face a picture of sad weariness, the boat violently dashed against the wind, throwing the lady forward. Sarah leaped to catch her, preventing the woman from falling down the staircase. "You might have been killed, Madame," she said.

"Yes, but it was not God's will," the woman answered.

Sarah Bernhardt in Sardou's early success, *Théodora*, a dramatic moment from the climax of the play (from the collection of Peter van der Waal).

Sarah magnanimously announced herself. "I am Sarah Bernhardt," she offered, expecting the woman to be happily stunned.

Instead, the woman pulled back and said in a sorrowful voice, "I am the widow of President Lincoln." She muttered something about God not wanting her to die just yet and quietly wandered away.

In her autobiography Sarah wrote, "I too recoiled, and a great sorrow overcame my entire being, for I had rendered this unhappy woman the one service she didn't want ... that of saving her from death. An actor had assassinated her husband, President Lincoln, and it was an actress who prevented her from rejoining him. I returned to my cabin and stayed there for two days, for I hadn't the courage to encounter this touching soul to whom I would never dared have spoken. I wept because I was touched, tired, unnerved, weary and in great need of repose. I fell asleep amid my tears, my bosom rising and falling with sighs and sobs." Mary Todd Lincoln never gave any account of her encounter with Sarah.

After a twelve-day crossing, the *L'Amérique* landed in New York harbor on a freezing cold morning. Sarah met bands playing the "Marseillaise" and U.S. customs inspectors. She had to endure endless rounds of press interviews, followed by a

Sarah Bernhardt in Sardou's *Théodora* (from the collection of Peter van der Waal).

tour of the Brooklyn Bridge and a public appearance at a performance of *Alixe*, starring Clara Morris.

Her opening performance was in *Adrienne Lecouvreur* on November 8, playing to a packed house of New York City's richest curiosity seekers. Sarah did not appear during the first act, and impatient audience members began demanding their tickets refunded. When the second act appeared, it began with Sarah reciting the poem of "The Two Pigeons." "Instead of the hysterical skeleton that had been announced to them, they had before them a very frail-looking creature with a sweet voice," Sarah wrote. By the time her character was dying in the fifth act, poisoned by her rival, there was "quite a manifestation and everyone was deeply moved," according to Sarah.

Sarah gave twenty-seven performances in New York. Before leaving that city, Jarrett had arranged a short trip to Menlo Park to the residence of Thomas Edison. It was on this dark night Sarah's path crossed that of the man whose inventions ultimately gave her the immortality she always wanted. As her carriage pulled through the falling snow to Edison's home, the electric lights were suddenly illuminated from the trees, among the bushes and along the garden walks. As lights flashed forth, Sarah and her touring group drew up at the house, searching the faces of their greeters for Mr. Edison. "I noticed the flush that came into the face of one of them," Sarah said, "and it was so evident from the expression of his blue eyes that he was intensely bored. I guessed this was Edison." Sarah immediately marveled at meeting Edison and followed him and his wife up staircases and across bridges on a tour of his laboratory facilities. "I understood all, and I admired him more and more, for he was so simple and charming, this king of light," she said. Thomas Edison demonstrated the telephone and the phonograph for Sarah. She recorded a short excerpt from *Phèdre* onto the early tin-foil recording machinery and listened to the playback of her voice through the horn of the playing machine, marveling at the miracle of the sound reproduction.

The tour took them through the Americas and into Canada on board the "Sarah Bernhardt Special," consisting of three Pullmans for the personnel and her own private car. The scenery and costumes were sent ahead on freight express, and all tracks were cleared along the way for the entourage. It was a brutal schedule of one-night stands, often arriving only hours before a curtain and departing immediately after for the next town. By the time the train returned to New York she had given 157 performances in 51 cities.

Sarah returned to Paris, where a cult had developed from a public who collected her photographs and press notices. While she was away, they had been soaking up every rumor spread by the insatiable press. She went on a tour of England, followed by an extended tour of Italy, Greece, Hungary, Switzerland, Belgium, Holland, Germany, and Russia. The Bernhardt legend had spread over the entire world wherever she went to perform. Crowds came whether or not they understood a word that she spoke. She gave command performances to crowned heads of state in their palaces.

For a time Sarah performed in Paris, then went on another whirlwind tour the length and breadth of South America in a repertory of plays.

In 1891 Sarah went on a two-year tour, which took her halfway around the world and back again. This time she performed a repertory of fifteen productions, dragging tons of scenery and costumes through every major city that hosted a theater. It was during this tour she suffered an injury to her knee while in a performance of *La Tosca*, severely harming herself for the rest of her life. At the end of the play her character leaps to her death from a ledge onto some mattresses hidden from the au-

Sarah brandishing an ax in a striking photograph taken by Felix Nadar.

dience's view. The stage had not been set properly, and Sarah struck her knee on the bare boards of the stage. She was barely able to walk for days but managed to continue to act despite the great pain.

In 1893 Sarah bought the Théâtre de la Renaissance, which she renamed Théâtre Sarah Bernhardt, for 700,000 francs and there produced sumptuous plays under her personal supervision. During the first five years she produced nine plays, three of which were big hits. Audiences reveled in her presentations of *Les Rois, Phèdre, Magda, Lorenzaccio, Gismonda* and *La Dame aux Camélias*.

In 1899 Sarah created an unusual production of *Hamlet* in French. Word of this

Left: Sarah in 1899 in the Paris production of *Hamlet*, translated by Marcel Schwob and Eugène Morand. *Above:* Sarah with Yoric's skull in 1899 in the Paris production of *Hamlet*, an interpretation that received world-wide press for the unique characterization of Sarah playing the melancholy Dane.

unorthodox presentation received worldwide press. Rarely did a woman successfully perform Shakespeare's play, but Sarah made a unique characterization out of the role of Hamlet, and her effort was highly respected and admired by those who saw it.

L'Aiglon, by Edmond Rostand, was first read to Sarah at the Théâtre Sarah Bernhardt. She fell in love with the play, and in 1900 it burst onto the theatrical world with all the fireworks of the new millennium. The script was full of patriotic speeches that gave Sarah full vent for the kind of declamatory vocalizations for which she was justly famous. The play was a sensation in Paris and the hit of the following season in London. Sarah took the play on her sixth tour of the United States, bringing with *L'Aiglon* other popular plays such *as Cyrano de Bèrgèrac, Hamlet, La Tosca* and *La Dame aux Camélias.*

She spent the summer on her beloved island called Belle Isle, a secluded country estate she had purchased some time before as the need for an annual respite grew. Sarah's summers on the island were immortalized in the two-reel film *Sarah Bernhardt à Belle Isle*, also known as *Sarah Bernhardt at Home.* This film was exhibited in many towns where she played on successive tours, trading on the publicity of her live performances and bringing cash into budding movie theaters called nickelodeons.

At the Théâtre Sarah Bernhardt she continued to produce one sumptuous exhibition after another, including the final play by Victorien Sardou *La Sorcière*, a turgid drama full of slick dialogue, incredible situations, and theater that enthralled audi-

Left: Sarah as the Duc de Reichstadt in Rostand's *L'Aiglon* in 1900, one of her greatest successes. *Above:* Another scene of Sarah as the Duc de Reichstadt in Rostand's *L'Aiglon* in 1900. Her role as the son of Napoleon was courageous as she was then fifty-six years old.

ences with her role of Soraya, a gypsy accused of sorcery and condemned to die at the stake. At the age of fifty-nine Sarah played eight performances a week and frequently added special matinees of plays such as *Andromache* and *Esther*.

The big hit of the 1905 season in London was *Pelléas et Mélisande,* a play by Louis Maeterlinck. Sarah played the male lead opposite Mrs. Patrick Campbell.

Sarah Bernhardt's farewell tour of 1905-1906 again took her across the United States, where she was forced to play in circus tents. The all-powerful Theatrical Syndicate closed most of the theaters and opera houses to her throughout the country because Sarah refused to pay their inflated fees. She reacted by erecting a special round-top tent created by her managers to allow her to appear before thousands of people at each show. This gave her theatrical evenings the air of a circus event, and Sarah was delighted with the adventure. She set up near local

Sarah Bernhardt performing in an outdoor amphitheater in *Phèdre* at the Hearst Greek Theater on May 17, 1906.

fairgrounds beside hastily laid railroad lines that rolled the thousands of spectators directly to the performances.

In 1907–1910 she produced many original plays at her theater in France, spending eighteen hours a day at her theater and going on repeated tours with the hits. The pain in her knee, injured during the earlier Rio de Janeiro stage accident, had become anguishing. Walking was difficult, and her stage movements were frequently done with the aid of another character placed carefully on her arm.

Sarah had become a worldwide institution. The movies had already captured her in a one-reel version of *La Tosca*, and she followed this with the film that was to give her the immortality she craved, the 1912 *Queen Elizabeth*. With her in this film was the young man who was to be the one actor most closely identified with her experiments in motion pictures.

Lou-Tellegen

At the age of sixty-six Sarah's second farewell tour of 1910 took her across America with a new leading man, Lou-Tellegen, a tall, extremely handsome man whose powerful build made him ideal as Armand Duval and most of the other leading male parts in her repertory of plays.

Lou-Tellegen, Sarah's leading man on her seventh and third from final American tour of 1910. Mr. Tellegen was thirty-one playing opposite Sarah at sixty-six.

"I had never met, nor have I met to this day, another human being from whom personality emanated so richly as from that divine person," wrote Lou-Tellegen about Sarah Bernhardt. "I had faced almost everything in life — danger, death, horror, murder, love, despair — but I must admit that, however my emotions had become steeled through all the risks of my perilous existence, my heart seemed to stand still for a moment when I faced that immortal creature."

Sarah Bernhardt entered motion pictures at an advanced age, facing the same difficulties that all performers who are well past their youth have endured since films began. As movies told stories in terms of youth, Sarah wisely surrounded herself with young actors in order to maintain this focus on youth.

Lou-Tellegen was her leading man in *Queen Elizabeth, La Tosca* and *Camille*, the three films that began her initial success in the new medium. He was a tall, chiseled, former circus acrobat who had a physical grace and striking appearance that burned through the images of early celluloid film. His features played against those of the older Bernhardt in a highly complementary fashion and had much to do with the success of these three motion pictures. His bonding with early nickelodeon audiences was so strong that these three films with Sarah Bernhardt led directly to a film career lasting from 1911 to his death in the early 1930s.

Lou-Tellegen was born in the Castle de Hulst at St. Oedenrode in the south of Holland, on November 26, 1881. This was at the time that Sarah Bernhardt was at the pinnacle of her fame in the theater. The son of a Dutch dancer and a Greek military general, he grew up in the wealthy life in the Royal Palace at the time of Queen Wilhelmina.

At the age of 15 he ran away from home with his father's favorite *belle amie*, a nineteen-year-old Russian with whom Lou was madly in love. They journeyed to Berlin for a few weeks and then took a train to St. Petersburg, where he thrived on the vitality of a magnificent Russian home life with her family. Their love affair quickly extinguished itself, leaving Lou to face the world alone for the first time in his life.

He fell prey to conniving publishers of a book on birth control, having accepted a salesman position for a book that contained twelve startlingly realistic colored plates showing a woman's body from the first to the last stage of childbirth. Police quickly arrested the naïve salesman, throwing him into a dirty, smelly, stone-walled cell for months. After a short trial proved him to be innocent of the book's manufacture, Lou found himself free from prison and in the companionship of a beautiful Slavic woman six years his senior. In his autobiography, *Women Have Been Kind*, Lou described her as "the essence of all that love can give to one in the prime of youth."

This woman found work as a newspaper journalist in Moscow. Her writings were of a nature that local authorities considered to be treasonous, and she was arrested and accused of being a spy and a dangerous anarchist. Lou was arrested along with her and again found himself in a filthy Russian prison for two weeks before being acquitted.

His lady, however, was condemned for life in the salt mines in the wilderness of Siberia. Once again, Lou wandered for weeks from town to town as he made his way toward Germany.

In a bakery in Wollstein, Germany, Lou met his next love, the wife of the owner of the bakery. After being trained for one month, he fell in love with the owner's wife, only to discover her beaten unconscious by her husband during a drunken rage. Lou tended her wounds and consoled her in an idyll that lasted only until the outraged husband surprised the two of them one afternoon while in the act of consolation. Lou boarded the first train to Posen and then entered into a series of circumstances that would shape the remainder of his life.

Although Lou had been on the stage with his mother as early as five years of age, he had not pursued a career in the theater until he stumbled into a fortuitous relationship with a young actress of Hungarian

Lou-Tellegen in 1917 in a studio portrait taken while he was starring in silent films in America.

descent, the rage of Berlin and Vienna theaters in the early nineteenth century. Lou attended a festival with the young actress that climaxed with a stage presentation in a ballroom that had been transformed into a theater. That night Lou witnessed a play for the first time in his life, and the experience left an indescribable impression on his soul. He asked himself, "Was it possible that these same men and women I had met in the afternoon had transformed themselves into the flesh and blood of others? My inherited vocation was calling to my blood. It aroused me from the dangerous and unimportant life I had been leading. I began to conserve my energy for a more worthy cause than the roaming existence of a vagabond."

The splendors of the festival lasted until the following day. Lou met the actors and approached them about his intention of becoming an actor. The young actress who had led him to the festival asked him, "So you would like to join my company and become an actor?"

Every word she spoke made him tremble with emotion. "Yes, I have made up my mind. I want to be on the stage, to act beside you, no matter how small the part might be," he exclaimed.

She smiled at his enthusiasm and naïve manner. "I will think it over," she said. With an elegant gesture, she flicked his cheek with a fan, smiled and walked away.

The next day he left with the train carrying her company toward his destiny as an actor. For six months he climbed from being an ordinary actor in minor parts to the position of the leading man of the company. But the ambitious actress soon tired of her fling with the young actor and replaced him with another actor who was able to further her career goals. Lou lost the relationship and his job with the company.

Many months later, while passing through the suburbs of Berlin, Lou noticed the crudely colored posters of a circus that was appearing in the area. He attended the daily performance for a week and became immensely impressed by the acrobats on the flying trapeze. When the circus broke tent and left for Frankfurt, Lou followed them.

He begged the acrobats to teach him the secrets of their art, and they agreed to break him into the rhythmic swings of airborne somersaults. He trained for weeks in rehearsal while on their road tour, until the star performer suddenly left for a more tempting offer with another circus. His vacancy opened up the opportunity for Lou to join the remaining two strong men of the act called "The Three Bernard Brothers." His triumph as a flying trapeze artist was the result of a stringent, severe exercise and diet routine administered by the two strong men who watched over Lou as if he were their own son.

In the circus was a lovely young German girl, about nineteen years of age and an expert cyclist with the circus. As would be expected, he became intimately involved with the stuntwoman, and had he stayed with the circus, he would have been content with a career in the circus. But fate intervened and ended his success with an injury during a flight. In the middle of a performance, when he took a full swing, Lou timed one of the somersaults wrong by a split second and missed the grip on the wrist of one of the partners. He landed in a corner of the net, which snapped and dropped him to the arena floor. He suffered only a broken foot, but the act was immediately cancelled. Lou again found himself alone in Hanover as the circus passed away and out of his life.

Lou next became an artist's model, selling his acrobat's body to sculptors in Brussels. He made a living posing naked for entire days, earning francs from painters and sculptors until he could save enough to realize his dream to go to Paris and continue studies in the artistic world of the theater.

With a letter of recommendation to the famous artist Rodin, Lou ventured into

Lou-Tellegen with his wife, Metropolitan Opera diva Geraldine Farrar, in Hollywood, where they starred in silent films such as *The Woman and the Puppet*.

Paris. About his first view of the boulevards, he wrote, "I was inspired. I felt like a young man who owned the world and I saw sincerely that for the first time in my life I felt at home. That city with its glamour and warmth seemed to take me to its bosom, and its magic voice sang in my ears." Soon, the magic voice of Sarah Bernhardt would also sing in his ears, as Lou was destined to cross paths with the great woman who would be the force that changed his life forever.

Auguste Rodin, a robust man with a grayish beard and unkempt hair, received Lou with the letter of recommendation and, after studying him, hired him to pose for his works. Lou studied drama while working under the wing of Rodin. After posing for many sketches and statues, he left with the artist's blessing and the following morning arrived to face life in Paris.

He met Loie Fuller at the peak of her fame. She was preparing a famous production of *Salomé* to be performed in dance and pantomime, and she engaged Lou to play John the Baptist. After months of studying under the tutelage of Paul Mounet, Lou auditioned for the distinguished board of the Conservatoire, France's leading training ground for students of the theater. He was one of the few foreigners accepted and soon established himself as a promising actor.

He graduated from the Conservatoire and was engaged at the Theatre de l'Odeon under the direction of André Antoine. After months of Lou's performing, a friend sent a message to Maurice Bernhardt, son of Sarah Bernhardt, introducing Lou to the divine Sarah. Her manager had been looking for him for months, as Sarah had seen him several times at the Odéon Theater and requested him to join her company as her leading man on a forthcoming tour of America.

"Eternal Springtime" by Auguste Rodin. Lou-Tellegen posed for this statue, the original of which is in the Metropolitan Museum of Art, New York.

Lou wrote, "After being announced I felt my heart beating a little faster when I knocked at the door of her drawing-room in the Carlton Hotel. The door opened and there stood in the doorway a creature from Heaven! Her gown was of white lace; her eyes seemed like stars. Her personality was overwhelming. Yes, I understood now why that gorgeous woman had the power to hold a world spellbound!" Sarah looked about twenty, although she was well on in years, and Lou was dazzled by the sparkling en-

Sarah with Lou-Tellegen in *Théodora* during a performnace on one of their many tours during 1910 to 1913.

thusiasm she displayed as she invited him to come back later that day for lunch and to discuss business.

When again he entered her home, a table was set for three. The lunch and the conversation entranced him. "I could not repress my astonishment during these moments that this woman, who was then nearly sixty-nine years of age, had the spirit, looks and vivacity of a girl of twenty," he claimed.

Sarah with Lou-Tellegen in the motion picture *Queen Elizabeth* in 1912. His role as Lord Essex is the one for which he is most remembered.

After dinner, Sarah got up and disappeared into her private room. When she reappeared later, she carried some papers and began to talk in a very businesslike manner about contracts, salaries, money, travel, and routes. She explained that she had drawn up a contract for a weekly salary and that it called for Lou's services for four years with fifty-two consecutive weeks' salary per year. "Please read this over, Monsieur Tellegen, and if the contract suits you, please sign it. We leave for America in ten days."

Never in his life had he earned so much money. "A salary? A king's ransom," he remembered. "I equaled it only when I did pictures in Hollywood a few years ago. For a stage salary in 1910 it was unheard of." Lou tore up the contract, saying, "Your word is enough. That is a contract, not these papers."

Sarah looked at him for a moment and there was silence. She rose and finally said, "You accept?"

Lou accepted, and spent the following ten days memorizing a dozen roles in the repertoire for the American tour.

After a year of touring in the United States, the entourage returned to France. Sarah opened her new season with a play written especially for her, *Queen Elizabeth*. Although the whole production was magnificent, the critics and the public did not receive it favorably, and the play was forced to close. Sarah lost a great deal of money on it but salvaged the ruin by agreeing to make a motion picture of the same title from it. "I believe it was the first four-reel picture with a story ever made," Lou recalled. "The French film company broached the subject to me, and Sarah thought I was mad when I begged her to do it. It was only after weeks of swearing, 'Never!' that she finally gave in and we went to work."

Lou recalled that the camera did not move but photographed everything from the same position. The moment it was released it began to make money for the American company distributing the film. Ultimately the owners made a fortune from it in the United States and abroad. Lou-Tellegen also made his fortune in silent movies, for this film brought him offers that took him away from Sarah to star alone. She said to him, "Be wise, my child. Learn English. They like you in America. There is your future. Go first to England and after that, return to the United States."

"At this time, I met a man who had attained tremendous fame and fortune in the motion picture world of today, and I wish to state emphatically that his success is wholly due to his own dashing, energetic, indomitable will and keen foresight. I mean Samuel Goldwyn," Lou remembered. "He was then with the Lasky Film Company and he engaged me as a star." His marriage to Geraldine Farrar, the great opera star, may have had more than a little influence on his sudden success in films.

Lou starred in his first film, *The Explorer*. Other films followed, including *The World and Its Woman*, *The Puppet* and *The Flame of the Desert*.

He signed a contract with Vitagraph and made *Let Not Man Put Asunder* with Pauline Frederick; *The Redeeming Sin* with Alla Nazimova; *Between Friends* with Anna Q. Nilsson and many more. He also directed several pictures for Vitagraph and Fox.

His last wife, Eva Casanova, said of him, "Forty-seven years ago when he was born, he was the infant of what might be called the 'brilliant age of France.' Those who influenced him were the greatest sages and the most beautiful women of the world. He has owned palaces and slept on park benches; eaten peacocks' tongues and starved; been a fencer, pugilist, sculptor, bullfighter, playwright and actor, to mention only his outstanding professions."

Lou-Tellegen committed suicide in 1933, dying alone. Almost all of his motion pictures have been lost, and of the few surviving titles, the three he made with Sarah Bernhardt have given him a measure of immortality. His portrayal of Lord Essex in *Queen Elizabeth* is the role for which he is remembered.

Quand Même

Headlines around the world expressed genuine empathy for Sarah when her leg had to be amputated in February of 1915. P. T. Barnum, who was then touring his freak show around the country, had the effrontery to offer her $10,000 for the exclusive right to display the severed leg in his exhibition. Sarah declined his offer. She convalesced as the public speculated how she could ever play on stage again.

She immediately made a film of *Jeanne*

Doré, followed by an appearance in a one-act play called *Les Cathédrales* by Eugène Morand. Sarah appeared in a tableau enthroned on a dais, declaiming a long speech, and then for effect, raised herself into a standing position to ring out her final, powerful exclamation. She proved that she was far from finished.

In 1913 she went on yet another farewell tour, playing in vaudeville in single scenes from her most famous plays. An

Quand Même, Sarah Bernhardt's personal logo and symbol of her attitude toward life.

amusing account by Percy Hammond details a typical Bernhardt vaudeville day: "After the stage hands swept away the debris caused by the preceding song and dance exhibition, the band, with some impressiveness, played the "Marseillaise" over and over again, and then the curtain went up. Madame Sarah entered a bit wearily, and leaned upon the arm of that none too ducal throne of the palace of Ferrara, the third act of *Lucrezia Borgia*. The people of the midwest arose to the event rather conventionally, applauding about half as much as their applause for Miss Eva Tanguay on her first appearance. Madame Sarah makes no secret of the fact that she is sixty-nine, and neither does [*sic*] her costumes. She is sixty-nine and looks it and her clinging to the scenery is rather pathetic. To those whose French is timid, her chant and intonations are as rhythmic, her rapid patter as helter-skelter, and her short, sharp, metallic strokes in diction as effective as they ever have been. This is no veteran lagging superfluous, but a

green old age, unconscious, or at least indifferent, of decays. The vaudeville audience is not a tender one and veneration is not among its characteristics. But it is very quiet while Madame Bernhardt performs, except when she becomes violent in her elocution, and then it applauds. It applauds, in fact, every bit of stormy recitation, outbursts being a safe hint for appreciation of acting in an alien tongue.

"She skims deftly over the more vehement emotions, and after dashing the louis d'or in Armand's face in *Camille*, for instance, she returns with tranquility at once to the wings, and the eating of an apple or the manicuring of her nails. She finds it easy to dispel precipitately the histrionic moods. The outcries of Sardou are to her nothing more than the outcries of Sardou. Even the yellow drama of her son Maurice, *A Christmas Night Under the Terror* results in no particular aftermath off stage. Hovering around her dressing room are a physician, a valet, a masseuse, three maids, a secretary, a personal representative, an interpreter, and a treasurer. This last named functionary seems to be fully as important as any of the others.

"At the risk of being iconoclastic, it may be reported that ere the tumult and the shouting dies, Madame Sarah's eager hands are pleasantly outstretched for her daily wage, which is paid to her each evening in fresh $100 bills. A crease in one of them is enough to cause its rejection. It appears that the overlords of vaudeville disburse $10,000 per week in behalf of this act, that sum including the salaries of her twenty-six players and their transportation between engagements."

In 1914 she toured the villages during the worst of World War I giving performances in barns, tents, hospitals, and makeshift stages. In 1916 she made another motion picture, *Les Mères Françaises*, filmed in the trenches and bombed villages of France.

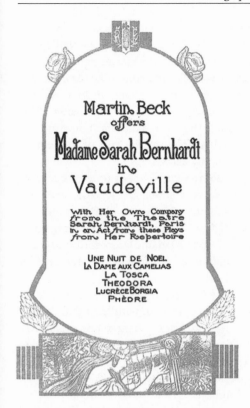

Madame Sarah Bernhardt in a vaudeville advertisement from promoter Martin Beck, ca. 1912.

Her final farewell American tour was a back-breaking, eighteen-month stint with scenes from her famous plays and new one-act plays. In *Au Champs d'Honneur*, a cleverly constructed vehicle for Sarah, she played a wounded soldier awakening from bombardment at the stump of a tree, searching for his misplaced flag and reciting patriotic speeches to a passing soldier. One of these, *A Prayer for Our Enemies*, was recorded on early 78rpm discs.

An article in the October 1915 *Theatre Magazine*, titled "Her American Manager," says, "She has created in herself a national figure, so that wherever Sarah Bernhardt appears, she personifies the flag of her country. She is the embodiment of the national ambition in France, which aspires to the highest culture, to unwavering courage, to infinite tenderness. Sarah is the heart and head of France."

Right, top: Sarah Bernhardt in vaudeville, ca. 1912, a studio portrait. *Right, bottom:* Sarah in 1923, a portrait taken for *Motion Picture World* magazine shortly before she died.

Sarah continued to tour in plays for the next few years in *Tout à Coup, Les Cathédrales, Daniel, La Gloire, Comment On Ecrit l'Histoire*, and *Régine Armand*. *Daniel* was filmed in 1921 using the style of silent movies, complete with titles inserted for the spoken dialogue and close-ups. Pathe Gazette distributed the film. It is not known whether the entire play was filmed or just the final scene, for the five minutes of existing footage show Sarah only in the powerful death scene, all the years of her life visible in garish, well-lit close-ups.

In *Sarah Bernhardt* (1931) Maurice Baring writes, "In November of 1922 she began a tour in Italy, which included performances at Marseilles, Genoa, Milan, Verona, Venice, Bologna, Florence, Rome and Turin. She was playing in M. Verneuil's two plays, *Daniel* and *Régine Arman* and on the 17th of November while traveling by motor-car going from Marseilles to Genoa, her motor collided with a lorry." She was not injured, but the motorcar could no longer be used. She was now always carried about in a chair, and she had to have a mo-

torcar especially constructed to carry this chair. After this accident she was obliged to travel by train. This meant going to a new town every day and getting up sometimes at six o'clock in the morning for long and tiring journeys involving many changes. She finished the tour with difficulty and returned to Paris at the end of November thoroughly exhausted.

Back in Paris she began to rehearse *Un Sujet de Roman*. She attended all of the rehearsals but became very ill from uremia on the night of the dress rehearsal. Sarah's part was given to Madame Reggers to study, and the play was postponed to a later date for production.

In January of 1923 she regained her strength and signed, with her usual zeal for a new production, a contract to appear in a motion picture titled *La Voyante* for an American firm, to be produced by Louis Mercanton, the director of *Queen Elizabeth*. Filming began and progressed until the beginning of March, when her condition again worsened. The studio moved the sets into her home and she continued to work. Ac-

Tens of thousands of people crowded the streets of Paris at Sarah's funeral in 1923.

Three views of the funeral procession, where all of Paris paid homage to their great artist Sarah Bernhardt.

Top: The funeral service at Cathédrale de Westminster. *Middle:* The procession passing the Théâtre Sarah Bernhardt. *Foreground:* Interior of the Cathédrale de Westminster.

Sarah in the Bettini Recording Laboratory, listening to one of her dramatic recitations on the wax cylinder phonograph.

Sarah Bernhardt's grave (from the collection of Peter van der Waal).

cording to Maurice Baring, "So great was her vitality that on Sunday night the *Times* correspondent telegraphed to London that in the doctor's opinion there was no immediate danger, and recovery was even possible." Sarah had inquired whether her coffin, which she had ordered years before, was in order, and had joked with the doctors.

The next day, on Monday the 26th, her condition changed for the worse. A few more takes were filmed of Sarah before she collapsed from the uremia. After a priest gave her the last sacraments the following morning, she sank into a coma and died that evening. She was buried at the Père Lachaise and given a magnificent funeral. Photos and motion picture newsreels taken at the event show the streets of Paris filled with people as far as the eye could see.

Part 2
SOUND RECORDINGS

Introduction

The magical, snowy night when Sarah Bernhardt visited the home of Thomas Edison was the beginning of what would be the first in a number of recordings she made. As is so often the case with beginnings, Sarah's first recording session was a casual encounter, with no advance preparation and certainly no thought of how useful the recording would be to future generations.

Of all his inventions, Thomas Edison felt the most fondness for the phonograph. The telegraph and the telephone were two of his other inventions that led to a way to record sound on tinfoil-coated cylinders in 1877. In 1878 Edison's attention was transferred to the incandescent light bulb, and he set aside his work on the phonograph. During that time of distraction, other inventors improved on his invention. Chichester A. Bell and Charles Sumner Tainter were two who developed a wax cylinder for the phonograph, which Edison used when he resumed work on his machine. The initial use for the invention was as a dictating machine for offices, but the phonograph quickly became a popular form of entertainment. Edison's company eventually provided recording selections in a variety of formats to the public, introducing models that were improved over the years. The Blue Amberol Record,

featuring superior sound and an unbreakable material, ended his creativity on the invention. In 1912 the disc phonograph was developed to compete in the disc market, which had become the popular choice. The Edison Diamond Discs offered excellent sound and were designed to not compete with other players. In October of 1929, the day before the stock market crash, he ceased the production of records forever.

The early phonograph recordings were literally accomplished by force, all acoustically. The performers would stand before a funnel-shaped horn attached to a phonograph and belt out their speeches or tunes. High volumes of sound were required to force the recording diaphragm to vibrate sufficiently to force the cutting stylus to make a good carving onto the blank wax cylinder. Some instruments did not record well, such as the violin, and other instruments such as horns recorded best. Early inventories of recordings were made by huddling multiple phonographs near the performers. The phonographs would be operated simultaneously, and each would make a recording of the performance. The recorded cylinders would then be replaced with fresh blanks, and the process repeated. A band could make, in this fashion, from 10

41

Thomas Alva Edison, inventor of the phonograph, invited Sarah to Menlo Park in 1880 on her last day in America to see his inventions and make her first recording on the tin-foil phonograph.

to 15 recordings per take, repeating the performance for take after take. Soon, primitive duplicating methods were devised by connecting one phonograph to another, with a direct linkage that connected the reproducing stylus of the master to the recording stylus of the other phonograph.

Only a limited number of copies could be made using these techniques due to the degradation of the original wax recording. By mid–1902, cylinders could be copied by a molding process. This was a big improvement and cylinder prices dropped. At the same time, the wax itself was changed from a soft brown wax, which limited the playback lifetime of recordings, to a firmer black metallic soap-wax concoction.

All of Sarah's recordings are self-announcing, the title of the selection being named first, followed by her own name as the performer and the name of the author. This was a standard practice due largely to the lack of printed labeling on the early cylinder cases. By 1904 Edison began labeling his cylinders on their edge, and by 1909 most Edison recording were no longer self-announcing.

Sarah's first recording was done on the tin-foil device, a needle vibrating sound impressions onto strips of tin foil, the predecessor to household aluminum foil, wrapped around a 4-inch diameter drum. The drum

Left: Wax cylinder phonographs work in much the same way as disc phonographs: a sharp needle fits into the grooves carved into the cylinder, vibrating the sound waves into a bell that amplifies the sound (from the collection of Peter van der Waal). *Right:* This is a typical disc phonograph that plays flat recordings at 78 revolutions per minute, vibrating the sound waves into a bell that amplifies the sound (from the collection of Peter van der Waal).

was hand-cranked at about 60 revolutions per minute as the phonographic apparatus made sound impressions upon the foil. The expected lifetime of a foil recording was short because after a few playbacks the sound impressions were either worn down or the foil ripped. As of 2003 there has been no way to extract the sound from the surviving copy of her first recording, and Sarah's reading of a passage from *Phèdre* remains unplayed for 102 years.

Wax cylinders, like those featuring Sarah Bernhardt, were produced in colorfully labeled canisters (from the collection of Peter van der Waal).

Fortunately, her other recordings were made on wax cylinders. The cylinders were a little over two inches in diameter and four inches long, and they were brittle. Early wax cylinder recording speeds varied from as slow as 90 revolutions per minute, yielding approximately a two-minute recording, to faster speeds of from 120 to 160 revolutions for music that would run longer. Within a few years, phonographs were being sold for the home market, and by 1902 cylinder recording speeds were standardized to 160 rpm. By late 1908 4-minute cylinder recordings were available with a groove density doubled from the standard 100 to 200 grooves per inch. Edison continued making two-minute cylinders until late 1912.

Robert Feinstein, in an article called "Sarah Bernhardt and the Bettini Recording Legacy," in the February 2002 issue of *In the Groove*, wrote a fascinating description by Gianni Bettini of Sarah's work in his recording laboratory, quoting Bettini as having said,

> Here is Madame Sarah Bernhardt, photographed in this room, and in the act of listening to her voice from one of my machines, and no one could have suspected her identity until she began to declaim. Then she was superb, for she rightly took it as a

serious matter, this putting her voice on record for posterity.

These words were spoken, with distinct poetic license, by Lieutenant Gianni Bettini, as he proudly showed a reporter his framed picture of the actress. His words and her pictures were published in the May 18, 1899, issue of *Leslie's Weekly*, which described an encore visit by Bernhardt to Bettini's laboratory in 1896. The cylinders Madame Sarah made on that occasion were a passage from *Iziel* and *Un Peu de Musique*, the latter from a Victor Hugo work.

The *Leslie's* story exemplified an important aspect of the relationship between the inventor and Sarah Bernhardt, for she played a vital role in Bettini's emerging business. Her willingness to be repeatedly photographed with the lieutenant's inventions was much exploited, apparently with her consent, in his advertising campaigns. Bernhardt's likeness would appear in Bettini catalogs, on his posters, in his magazine advertisements, and in write-ups about his recording activities.

It was in December of 1891 or early 1892, when the actress first went to Lieutenant Bettini's studio, in Manhattan's Judge Building. Exactly how the visit was arranged might be a tale lost to history, but the best contemporary description of it appeared in *Leslie's Weekly* on March 3, 1892. And among the reasons why that magazine published several different accounts of Bernhardt recording for Bettini was one of access. Its headquarters were located at 110 Fifth Avenue, the Judge Building.

Gianni Bettini. The photograph is from the Robert Feinstein collection featured in *A Tribute to Gianni Bettini* (website http://www.talkingmachine.org/Bettini.html).

The article entitled, "The Phonograph and Its Improvements," included the following remarks: "The inventor's rooms in the Judge Building are daily visited by numbers of interested and scientific people. Among those who paid homage to the invention most recently is Sarah Bernhardt. Going up in the elevator like any ordinary every-day mortal, the greatest actress on earth entered Lieutenant Bettini's studio and quietly seated herself before the phonograph, which had been warranted to repeat all the tones of her wonderful voice. 'Recite something,' invited the Lieutenant, and Sarah broke forth into one of the scolding scenes of *Frou Frou*. When she had finished, the Lieutenant sent the machine going and every shade of Sarah's voice was given perfectly. The artist was so pleased that she declared she would own such a phonograph for the sake of hearing her own tones as others heard them."

Next day she came and was photographed before the phonograph. The tube was raised to her ear, and she started back in amazement at the wonderful sounds which issued from the voice of the trumpet.

The visit was a great success. A year from now, when Sarah wishes to know how her voice used to sound, she can reproduce the phonograph and hear herself exactly as she was.

When in New York, Bernhardt received ever-so-many invitations to visit various social gatherings and receptions, to see all sorts of curiosities, in the way of people and things, but Lieutenant Bettini is the only person who has had the honor of receiving Bernhardt in his own private little sanctum.

Most of Sarah's recordings have been located, and most of these have been transferred to modern LP, tape and CD technologies for the enjoyment of a new generation of her admirers. Her last series of recordings was made on discs, and their longer 3–4 minute lengths give a wonderful sense of the style of the plays as she performed with other actors, offering more than a fleeting glimpse of the performances.

No one at the time foresaw the possibilities of the recording technology. No full-length plays from her repertory were ever transferred in complete form onto records, and no one among her circle of writers and artists thought to blaze a new trail by creating an original drama just for the growing home theater market. What she recorded was poems and partial scenes from her plays.

These recordings capture both the higher key of her youthful voice and the slightly lower key of her older voice. In her final 1918 recording of *La Prière pour Nos Ennemis (The Prayer for Our Enemies)*, made five years before her death, we can hear that Sarah retained the musical delivery, unique vibrato and dramatic phrasing that made her world famous.

There are few actresses on the stage

today who can compete with the power of her delivery or the raw emotion radiating from her intonation. These recordings give us an opportunity to study her style and that of the French theater at the turn of the century.

Sarah performed exclusively in the French language. Although she played in many countries to audiences who couldn't understand a word of the plays, the stories were often quite well known. Those she had performed for decades had been copied by many others, and keeping an audience tuned to the proceedings was not difficult. For those who needed a translation, a copy of each play was generally available in a printed version with French and English beside each other on facing pages. Sarah often wearied of the interruption caused by the sound of the pages in the hands of playgoers turning in unison, a massive paper ruffling wafting up over the footlights while she was in the middle of a speech. She once lamented that the actors were forced to interject pauses into their dialogue to allow for the tumult of turning pages to cease.

In an article in *Movie Magazine*, January, 1926 (vol. 1, no. 5), titled "Sarah Bernhardt, A Memory," her godson, Gaston Glass, wrote,

A little slave boy bore in his brown hands a basket which held a snake. Cleopatra waited, her great eyes like jade in her white face — and all the audience held their breathing for a moment when she would take the asp and its green jeweled length would writhe as though it were alive. It looked alive in her hands, so that always the little boy, in his costume that was hardly more than his own brown skin, would catch his own breath and his eyes would grow big. I know, for I was that boy when Sarah Bernhardt was

Bettini Micro-Phonograph poster celebrated the renowned artists who recorded on his wax cylinders. Rod Cornelius took the original photograph of this poster for Robert Feinstein's website *A Tribute to Gianni Bettini* (http://www. talkingmachine.org/Bettini.html).

the greatest Cleopatra the world had ever seen.

She was my godmother. Her ear was wonderful, the least inflection off the perfect tone of a word and she would cry, "Stop! Stop! Try again. It must sound as…" and she would repeat the offending word with her own inflection, that perfect diction that made music of the slightest phrase. Purity was one of the first requisites of great acting. Madame demanded it, and would be satisfied with nothing less. "You will have dialect roles," she would tell [those of] us [in] the company, "and when you have to play in dialect, that is the time to use it. But at no other time. Your foundation must be on the purest of sound, and then you are free to put on what dialect you need for any

G&T pressing of *La Samaritaine* on Black GC-31171, Stamper II (courtesy of Kurt Nauck, of Nauck's Vintage Records, www.78rpm.com).

part. And it will be untainted by your natural pronunciation," she admonished.

Many actors and actresses have wondered where lay the secret of her great acting, as if it were something miraculous. In a way, perhaps, it was miraculous. But it was not a secret. It was simply that in each of her roles she was not acting — she was living. She was Camille, frail and passion-torn; she was the fate-laden boy, L'Aiglon, son of Napoleon; she was Jeanne, the maid of Orleans."

That was how she taught me. "You must feel everything — everything that you play. You cannot pretend. It must be real. Not only in the gesture or the voice, but all, the heart, the body, the words, everything!" she would say.

Sarah's perfect voice, intonation and pronunciation are evident in her sound recordings. She plays over the words like a musician plays an instrument, using beautiful pitch, intonation and vibrato as would a gifted singer.

There have been criticisms in various works about Sarah's choice of subjects for her recordings. The new English/French translations clearly reconcile concerns expressed about the choice of subjects. They seem perfect for Sarah's peculiar, ethereal artistry. Hearing these recordings, enlightened by the translations, aligns the listener with her artistic vision.

These new translations were accomplished by Professor Alissa Webel and Sheila Soman. They dug into the battered remains of the wax cylinder and disc recordings, transcribing the spoken French and superbly translating the words into modern English with moving and eloquent accuracy. Their labor was like dusting the ash off the fragile bones of skeletons buried and forgotten for eons. These two women deciphered the ancient recordings that have been seldom heard during the last hundred years, revealing Sarah's vocal power etched into the black wax of the whirling cylinders and discs.

Professor Webel described the effort as a difficult encounter. "Part of the problem was simply the overall surface noise of the old recordings covering Sarah Bernhardt's voice," she said. "Other times, she seems to say a word under her breath, or to swallow it, and thus even by bringing the sound up to a maximum, it appeared to not have been properly recorded initially. Other moments she speaks so fast that I was unable to understand what she was saying. Lastly, there were a few times when what I heard changed each time I listened to it. I could understand the vowels, but the consonants were not as clear, and when dealing with words that sound alike, and all potentially correct as far as the meaning goes, I preferred to leave it inaudible rather than provide a wrong transcript."

"Sarah's accent wasn't really much trouble for me," Professor Webel noted. "I love listening to Edith Piaf, who had a similar accent. French has evolved in its pronunciation since the beginning of the 20th century, with the main rupture being World War One. The least clear was definitely *L'Etoile dans la Nuit*, and the most difficult, because of the rhythm, was *Les Bouffons*. Having two recordings of *Le Lac* allowed me to overcome the few words I was having difficulty hearing."

Hearing the recordings now, and understanding their meaning, is like discovering the long-lost stories behind dusty hieroglyphics buried on the walls within the chambers of some ancient Egyptian tomb.

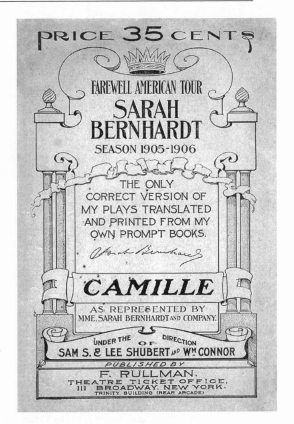

Sarah Bernhardt's managers provided audiences in countries speaking languages other than French with printed copies of the play with translations in both languages. The sound of hundreds of people turning pages in unison often upset the actors, forcing them to interject inappropriate pauses into their speeches. This *Camille* script sold for 35 cents in 1905.

Audiography

1880   ***Phèdre***
Written by Jean Racine
Recorded at Menlo Park, New Jersey, at the home of Thomas Edison
This performance is known to have survived, but the original tin-foil recording has proven to be to difficult to transcribe.

1896   ***Izeyl***
Written by Eugene Morand and Paul-Armand Silvestre
Recorded in New York at Bettini Phonograph Laboratory
Two minute wax cylinder
This performance is believed to be lost.

1902   ***La Fiancée du Timbalier***
Written by Victor Hugo
Recorded in Paris at Pathé Co.
Two minute wax cylinder

1902   ***Lucie***
Written by Alfred de Musset
Recorded in Paris at Pathé Co.
Two minute wax cylinder

1903   ***Le Lac (The Lake)***
Written by Maurice Bernhardt

Recorded in Paris
Two-minute wax cylinder
Black G&T 31170

1903   *La Samaritaine*
Written by Edmond Rostand
Recorded in Paris
72 rpm
Black G&T 31171

1903   *Les Vieux (The Old Ones)*
Written by Mme. Edmond Rostand
Recorded in Paris
72 rpm
Black G&T 31172

1903   *Un Evangel (A Gospel)*
Written by François Coppée
Recorded in Paris
72 rpm
Black G&T 31102

1903   *Phèdre*
Written by Jean Racine
Recorded in Paris
70 rpm
Black G&T 31103
Two-minute wax cylinder

1903   *La Mort d'Izail (The Death of Izail)*
Written by Maurice Bernhardt
Recorded in Paris
70 rpm
Black G&T 31104

1903   *Théroigne de Méricourt's Dream (Le Rêve de Théroigne de Méricourt)*
Written by Paul Ernest Hervieu
Recorded in Paris
78 rpm
10-inch light-blue Zonophone X-2129

1903   *Le Légende des Siècles, XV*
Written by Victor Hugo
Recorded in Paris
78 rpm
Light-blue Zonophone disc X-2130
This performance is believed to be lost.

1903   *Un Peu de Musique*
Also known as *La Chanson d'Eviradnus* (*The Song of Eviradnus*)
Written by Victor Hugo
Recorded in Paris at Zonophone Co.
Two-minute wax cylinder

1908   *Les Bouffons: La Brise Conte (The Breeze Tells)*
Written by Miguel Zamaçois

Recorded in Paris
16-inch Pathé disc

1910   *L'Aiglon: Act V, Scene V*
Written by Edmond Rostand
Recorded in West Orange, New Jersey
Four-minute Edison amberol cylinder 35007

1910   *Phèdre, Act II, Scene V*
Written by Jean Racine
Recorded in West Orange, New Jersey
Four-minute Edison amberol cylinder 35008 and 12-inch vertical-cut single sided disc. It is rumored that the voice of the actor in the part of Hippolyte is played in this recording by Lou Tellegen, based on the fact that he was prominent among the cast that toured America with Bernhardt in 1910 and played the role in the production at the time.

1910   *La Samaritaine: Act I, Scene V*
(Samaritan Encounters Jesus at the Wells of Jacob)
Recorded in West Orange, New Jersey
Four-minute Edison amberol cylinder

1918   *L'Etoile dans la Nuit (The Star in the Night)*
Written by Emile Guerinon and Henri Cain
Recorded in New York
78 rpm double-face vertical-cut disc
Acolian-Vocalion B22035

1918   *Prière pour Nos Ennemis (A Prayer for Our Enemies)*
Written by Louis Payen
Recorded in New York
78 rpm double-face vertical-cut disc
Acolian-Vocalion A22035

Above: Sarah Bernhardt ca. 1885, striking a pensive, melancholy mood. *Right:* Sarah Bernhardt modeling a traveling outfit, ca. 1880, from a postcard widely circulated around the world. She was the personification of French womanhood (photograph by Sarony).

La Fiancée du Timbalier (1902)

By Victor Hugo; recorded at Pathé
Translated by Sheila Soman

Monsignor, le Duc de Bretagne
a pour les combats meurtriers,
convoque de Nantes a Mortagne,
dans la plaine et sur la montagne,
l'arriere-ban de ses guerriers.

Ce sont des barons dont les armes
ornent des forts ceints d'un fosse;
des preux vieillis dans les alarmes,
des ecuyers, des hommes d'armes;
l'un d'entre eux est mon fiancé.

A Notre-Dame de Lorette
J'ai promis, dans mon noir chagrin,
d'attacher sur ma Gorgerette,
fermee a la vue indiscrete,
les coquilles du pelerine.

Mes soeurs, a vous parer si lentes,
venez voir pres de mon vainqueur,
ces timbales etincelantes
qui, sous sa main toujours tremblantes,
sonnent et font bondir le coeur!

Venez surtout le voir lui-meme
Sous le manteau que j'ai brode.
qu'il sera beau! c'est lui que j'aime!
Il porte comme un diademe
son casque de crins inonde!

L'Egyptienne sacrilege
M'attirant derriere un pilier,
m'a dit hier (Dieu nous protégé!)
qu'a la fanfare du cortege
il manquerait un timbalier.

Le Duc n'est pas loin: ses bannieres
flottent parmi les chevaliers;
Quelques enseignes prisonnieres,
honteuses, passent les dernieres...
Mes soeurs, voici les timbales!...

Monsignor, Duke of Brittany
has called together for deadly combat,
from Nantes to Mortagne,
in the plains and on the mountains,
the last of his warriors.

These are the barons whose arms
adorn those forts surrounded by moats,
aged shepherds all alarmed,
soldiers, men of arms;
and of them is my fiancé.

At Notre-Dame of Lorette
I've promised, in my dark despair,
to attach to my Georgette,
hidden from sight
the remnants of my travel.

My sisters, you who stop so lightly,
come near and see my conqueror,
these shining thimbles
that, within a hand always trembling,
sound and cause the heart to leap.

Come and see him yourself.
Under the coat that I've sewn,
how handsome he will be — it is he I love.
He carried a diadem
within the folds of his cap!

The pagan Egyptian
calls me behind a pillar,
told me yesterday (God have mercy!)
that in the parade of the troops
they are missing a timbalier.

The duke is not far, his banners
float among the chevaliers;
Several resigned prisoners,
shamed, bring up the rear.
My sisters, here are the timbaliers!

Elle dit, et sa vue errant	So she said, and her furtive eyes
plunge, heals! Dans les ranges presses;	lower, alas, among the crowded rows;
Pubis dans la foule indifferente,	Then, among an indifferent crowd,
elle tomba, froide et mourante…	she falls, cold and dying…
Les timbales etaient passes.	The timbaliers have passed.

Lucie (1902)

By Alfred de Musset; recorded at Pathé
Translated by Sheila Soman

Mes chers amis, quand je mourrai,	My dear friends, when I die,
plantez un saule au cimetière.	plant a willow in the cemetery.
J'aime son feuillage éploré.	I love the sad foliage.
La pâleur m'en est douce et chère,	The paleness is soft and dear,
et son ombre sera légère	and the shadow will be light
a la terre où je dormirai.	on the earth where I sleep.
Un soir, nous étions seuls,	One night, when we were alone,
j'étais assis près dell,	I was seated near her,
elle penchait la tête,	she lowered her head,
et sur son clavecin, laissait,	and on her harpsichord, while dreaming,
tout en rêvant, flotter sa blanche main.	let her white hand float.
Ce n'était qu'un murmure,	It was only a murmur, one would say,
on eût dit les coups d'aile d'un zéphyr	the beating of a wing of a zephyr
éloigné glissant sur des roseaux,	stretched out, gliding on the reeds
et craignant en passant	and fearing in passing
d'éveiller les oiseaux.	of wakening the bird.
Les tièdes voluptés des nuits mélancoliques	The voluptuous heat of melancholy nights
sortaient autour de nous du calice des fleurs.	leaving all around us a chalice of flowers.
Les marronniers du parc	The chestnut trees in the park
et les chênes antiques se berçaient	and the ancient oaks rock softly
doucement	
sous leurs rameaux en pleurs.	under their branches in tears.
La lune, se levant dans un ciel sans nuage.	The moon is rising in a cloudless sky.
D'un long réseau d'argent tout à coup	A long stream of silver suddenly fills it.
l'inonda.	
Elle vit dans mes yeux resplendir son image,	She lives in my eyes, taking in her image,
son sourire semblait d'un ange:	her angel-like smile:
elle chanta.	she sings.
Nous étions seuls, pensifs,	We were alone, pensive,
je regardais Lucie.	I looked at Lucie.

L'écho de sa romance
en nous semblait frémir.

Elle appuya sur moi sa tête appesantie.
Sentais-tu dans ton Coeur
Desdemona gémir, pauvre enfant?
Tu pleurais.

Sur ta bouche adorée
tu laissas tristement mes lèvres se poser,
et ce fut ta douleur
qui reçut mon baiser

Mes chers amis, quand je mourrai,
plantez un saule au cimetière.
J'aime son feuillage éploré.
La pâleur m'en est douce et chère,
et son ombre sera légère
a la terre où je dormirai.

The echo of the romance
seemed to make us shudder.

She leaned her head on me.
Do you feel in your heart
Desdemona groan, poor child?
You were crying.

On your sweet mouth
you sadly let me put my lips,
and it was your pain
that received my kiss.

My dear friends, when I die,
plant a willow in the cemetery.
I love the sad foliage.
The paleness is soft and dear,
and the shadow will be light
on the earth where I sleep.

Le Lac (The Lake) (1903)

Written by Maurice Bernhardt; recorded in Paris
Translated by Alissa Webel

Loin par-delà les mers,
sous le ciel des tropiques,
dans l'aube virginale
où s'endort la forêt,
sous l'enchevêtrement
des lianes antiques
brut, un trou glorieux de lumière apparaît.

Il s'élargit, dardant et brûlant les prunelles
comme un métal fondu qui bouille
sous le soleil;
et voila qu'au sortir
des gouttes éternelles,
c'est un lac, engourdi en son vaste sommeil.

Un lac de plomb, pesant et mort,
que rien ne trouble;
un lac dont nul frisson
ne terni le miroir,
et que caresse seul de son sillage double
le glissement furtif
des cygnes aux plumes noires.

Far beyond the oceans,
under the tropical skies,
in the virginal dawn
where the forest falls asleep,
under the entanglement
of the antique vines
a raw, glorious hole of light appears.

It widens, beaming and burning the eyes
as melted metal boils
under the sun;
and there, at the outlet
of the eternal drops,
is a lake, numbed in its long sleep.

A lake of lead, heavy and dead,
that nothing disturbs;
a lake of which no shiver
tarnishes the mirror,
and only caressed by the double wake
of the furtive glide
of the swans with black feathers.

Sur ses bords,
s'élançant et retombant par groupes,
tremblent de vastes lys
aux mystiques pâleurs;
et sur l'eau les lotus,
comme de larges coupes,
reçoivent par flocon les pétales des fleurs.

Et comme d'autres fleurs
qui passent autour d'elles,
mais vivantes,
des vols de papillons zébrés
remplissent l'air léger
d'un bruissement d'ailes
qui trouble au loin la paix
des silences sacrés.

Et la vie est partout,
si chaude et si puissante
que malgré moi,
je cherche au fond du ciel sans fin
a revoir dans l'azur
la trace encore présente
qu'y laissèrent les doigts
de L'ouvrier Divin.

On its borders,
leaping and falling by groups,
tremble large lilies
of mystical paleness;
and on the water the lotus,
like large cups,
receive by flakes the flower petals.

And like the other flowers
which go by around them,
but alive,
flights of tigered butterflies
fill the light air with
their batting wings
which disturbs in the distance
the sacred silences' peace.

And life is all around,
so warm and so powerful
that despite myself,
I seek in the depth of the endless sky
to see again in the blue
the trace still present
left by the fingers
of the Divine Worker.

Maurice Bernhardt, Sarah's son, wrote the haunting verses to *Le Lac*, recorded by his mother in 1903 as a gift to him. Photograph from the family album of Alain Campignon, Sarah's great-great grandson.

La Samaritaine (G&T 1903)

Translated by Sheila Soman

Il dit encore:

"Soyez doux. Comprenez. Admettez.
Souriez. Ayez le regard bon.
Ce que vous voudriez Qu'on vous fit,
que ce soit ce qu'aux autres vous faites:
Voila toute la loi,
voila tous les prophetes!
Envoyez votre Coeur souffrir dans
tous les maux!"

Enfin, que sais-je, moi!
Des mots nouveaux! Des mots
parmi lesquels un mot revient,
toujours le meme:
"Amour…amour…aimer!
Le ciel, c'est quand on aime.
Pour etre aimes du Pere,
aimez votre prochain.
Donnez tout par amour.
Partagez votre pain avec l'ami
qui vient la nuit, et le demande.

Si vous vous souvenez,
en faisant votre offrande,
Que votre frere a quelque chose
contre vous,
Sortez, et ne venez vous remettre
a genoux.
Qu'ayant, la paix conclue,
embrasse votre frere…
D'ailleurs, un tel amour,
c'est encor la misere.

Aimer son frere est bien,
mais un paien le peut.
Si vous n'aimez que ceux qui vous aiment,
c'est peu:
Aimez qui vous opprime
et qui vous fait insulte!
Septante fois sept fois pardonnez!
C'est mon culte
D'aimer celui qui veut decourager l'amour.

He says yet:

"Be kind. Understand. Admit.
Smile. Be of good heart.
That which you wish others to do to you,
do unto others:
That is the law,
that is all the prophecies!
Send your heart to suffer
among the evil!

Alas, what do I know!
New words. Only words
among which one keeps coming back,
always the same:
"Love…love…to love!
Heaven is to those who love.
To be loved by our Father,
love your neighbor.
Give all for love.
Share your bread with the friend
who comes in the night and asks.

If you remember,
in making your offer,
that your brother has done
something against you,
Go, and only come back
on your knees.
And by doing so, the peace accorded,
embrace your brother…
Besides, such a love,
there is still misery.

To love one's brother is good,
but a pagan could do it.
If you love those who love you,
it's only a little:
Love those who oppress you
and insult you!
Forgive seven fold!
That is my preaching,
to love those who discourage love.

S'il vous bat, ne criez pas contre, | If he beats you, do not cry against,
priez pour. | pray for.
S'il vous prend un manteau, | If he takes your mantle,
donnez-lui deux tuniques. | give him two tunics.
Aimez tous les ingrates | Love the ungrateful
commes des fils uniques. | as an only child.
Aimez vos ennemis, | Love your enemies
vous serez mes amis. | and you will be friends.
Aimez beaucoup, | Love even more,
pour qu'il vous soit beaucoup remis. | for it to be returned likewise.
Aimez encore. Aimez toujours. | Love still. Love forever.
Aimez quand meme. | Love despite all.
Aimez-vous bien les uns les autres. | Love you one another.
Quand on aime, | When one loves,
Il faut sacrifier sa vie a son amour. | One must sacrifice one's life to love.

Moi, je vous montrerai comment on aime, | I will show you how to love,
un jour… | one day…
Amour! | Love!
N'ayez que de l'amour dans la poitrine!… | Have nothing but love in your heart!…
Aimez-vous!" | Go forth and love!"

Above: Sarah Bernhardt in one of the last photographs taken, at the age of 79, shortly before she died on March 26, 1923. *Right:* Sarah Bernhardt in *La Samaritaine* by Rostand, in the role of Photine, ca. 1897 (from the collection of Peter van der Waal).

Les Vieux (The Old Ones) (1903)

Written by Mme. Edmond Rostand; recorded in Paris
Translated by Alissa Webel

Lorsque tu seras vieux et que je serais vieille,	When you will be old and I will be old,
lorsque mes cheveux blonds	when my blond hair
seront des cheveux blancs,	will be white hair,
au mois de Mai,	in the month of May,
dans le jardin tout en soleil,	in the garden full of sun,
nous irons réchauffer	we will go warm our
nos vieux membres tremblants.	old and trembling limbs.
Comme le renouveau mettra nos coeurs en fête,	As the renewal will cheer our hearts,
nous nous croirons encore	we will believe ourselves
de jeunes amoureux;	young lovers again;
et je te sourirais,	and I will smile to you,
tout en branlant la tête,	nodding my head,
et nous ferons	and we will form
un couple adorable de vieux.	an adorable old couple.
Nous nous regarderons,	We will look at each other,
assis sous notre treille,	sitting under our trellis,
avec de petits yeux attendris et brillants,	with small, tender and bright eyes,
lorsque tu seras vieux	when you will be old
et que je serais vieille,	and I will be old
lorsque mes cheveux blonds	when my blond hair
seront des cheveux blancs.	will be white hair.
Sur notre banc ami,	On our friend the bench,
tout verdâtre de mousse,	green with moss,
sur le banc d'autrefois,	on the bench of yesteryear,
nous reviendrons causer.	we will go back to talk.
Nous aurons une voix attendrie et très douce,	With a tender and soft voice,
la phrase finissant souvent	we will often finish a sentence
par un baiser.	with a kiss.
Combien de fois jadis	How many times before
j'ai pu dire "je t'aime?"	can I have said "I love you?"
Alors, avec grand soin,	Then, with great care,
nous nous re-conterons,	we will retell,
nous nous ressouviendrons de milles choses,	we will remember thousands of things,
même de petits rien, de tout dont	even little things and nothings
nous radoterons.	we will babble about.

Un rayon descendra d'une caresse douce	A ray will softly come down
parmi une mousse de blanc	among a cloud of white
et basier un rose et nouse se poser	and kiss a rose as we sit
sur notre banc amis,	on our friend the bench,
tout verdâtre de mousse,	green with moss,
sur le banc d'autrefois,	on the bench of yesteryear,
nous reviendrons causer.	we will go back to talk.
Et comme chaque jour je t'aime davantage,	And since every day I love you more,
aujourd'hui plus qu'hier	today more than yesterday,
et moins bien que demain,	less than tomorrow,
qu'importeront alors	what difference will the
les rides du visage?	wrinkles on our face make?
Mon amour,	My love,
ce sera si grave et si serein.	it will be so serious and serene.
Songe que tous les jours des souvenirs	Think that every day souvenirs embrace
s'enlacent c'est comme un souvenir	it is like a souvenir
toujours aimé plus.	always more cherished.
Et sans cesse entre nous	And ceaselessly between us
se tissent d'autres liens.	new ties weave.
C'est vrai nous serons vieux, très vieux.	It is true we will be old, very old.
Mais plus fort chaque jour	More strongly each day
je serrerai ta main	I will squeeze your hand
car vois-tu chaque jour	because, see, each day
je t'aime d'avantage,	I love you more,
aujourd'hui plus qu'hier,	today more than yesterday,
et moins bien que demain.	less than tomorrow.
Lorsque tu seras vieux et que je serais vieille,	When you will be old and I will be old,
lorsque mes cheveux blonds	when my blond hair
seront des cheveux blancs,	will be white hair,
au mois de Mai,	in the month of May,
dans le jardin tout en soleil,	in the garden full of sun,
nous irons réchauffer	we will go warm our
nos vieux membres tremblants.	old and trembling limbs.
Comme le renouveau	As the renewal
mettra nos coeurs en fête,	will cheer our hearts,
nous nous croirons encore	we will believe ourselves
de jeunes amoureux;	young lovers again;
et je te sourirais,	and I will smile to you,
tout en branlant la tête,	nodding my head,
et nous ferons	and we will form
un couple adorable de vieux.	an adorable old couple.

Nous nous regarderons,	We will look at each other,
assis sous notre treille,	sitting under our trellis,
avec de petits yeux attendris et brillants,	with small, tender and bright eyes,
lorsque tu seras vieux	when you will be old
et que je serais vieille,	and I will be old,
lorsque mes cheveux blonds	when my blond hair
seront des cheveux blancs.	will be white hair.

Sarah Bernhardt in the 1906 production of *La Vierge d'Avila*, in the role of St. Theresa.

Un Evangel (A Gospel) (1903)

Written by Francois Coppee
Translated by Alissa Webel

En ce temps-la Jésus, seul avec Pierre	In those days, alone with Peter,
errait sur la rive du lac près	Jesus wandered along the lake
de Nazareth.	near Nazareth.
A l'heure où le brûlant soleil de midi plane,	At the hour when the midday sun soars,
quand ils virent devant eux	when they saw before them
une pauvre cabane,	a poor shed,

la veuve d'un pécheur
en longs voiles de deuil,
qui s'était tristement assise sur le seuil,
retenant dans ses yeux,
la larme qui les mouille
pour bercer son enfant
et filer sa quenouille.

Non loin d'elle,
cachés par des figuiers touffus,
le Maître et son ami
voyaient sans être vus.

Soudain, un de ces gueux
dont le [inaudible] s'arrête
un mendiant portant un vase sur sa tête,
vint à passer et dit à celle qui filait:
"Femme, je dois porter ce vase
plein de lait chez un homme logé
dans le prochain village.
Mais, tu le vois, je suis faible
et brise par l'age.
Les maisons sont encore
à plus de mille pas
et je sens bien que seul je n'accomplirait pas
ce travail que l'on doit
me payer une obole."

La femme se leva sans dire une parole,
laissa sans hésiter sa quenouille de lin
et le berceau
d'osier où pleurait l'orphelin,
pris le vase, et s'en fut avec le misérable.

Et Pierre dit:
"Il faut se montrer secourable, Maître,
mais cette femme a bien peu de raison
d'abandonner ainsi son fils et sa maison
pour le premier venu qui s'en va sur la route,
ce vieux mendiant non loin d'ici
sans doute!
Quelque passant eut pris son vase
et lui eut porté!"

Mais Jésus répondit à Pierre:
"En vérité, quand un pauvre
a pitié d'un plus pauvre,

---

a fisherman's widow
in long mourning veils,
who was sadly sitting at the doorsill,
holding back the tear that wet her eye,
to rock her child and spin her distaff.

Not far from her,
hidden by dense fig trees,
the Master and his friend could see
without being seen.

Suddenly, a destitute one
came by and stopped,
a beggar carrying a vase on his head,
and said to the spinner:
"Woman, I must carry this vase
filled with milk to a man living
in the next village.
But, as you see, I am weak
and tired by age.
The houses are still more than
a thousand steps away
and I can feel I will never alone
accomplish this job for which
I am to be paid a coin."

The woman rose without a word,
left without hesitation her work
and the wicker crib
in which the orphan was crying,
took the vase, and left with the poor man.

And Peter said:
"One must be helpful, Master,
but this woman has little sense
to so abandon her son and house
for the first passerby on the road,
this old beggar, not far from here
I am sure!
Someone passing would have
taken the vase and carried it for him!"

But Jesus answered Peter:
"In truth, when a poor man
takes pity on a poorer man,

mon Père veille sur sa demeure
et son fils.
Cette femme a bien fait
de partir sans surseoir."

Quand il dit ses mots,
le seigneur vint s'asseoir
sur le vieux banc de bois
devant la vielle hutte et, d'une main,
pendant une minute, il fila la quenouille
et berça le petit.

Puis se levant,
Il fit signe à Pierre et partit.
Et quelle revint à son logis,
la veuve a qui de sa bonté
Dieu donnait cette preuve, trouva
sans deviner jamais par quel ami,
sa quenouille filée et son fils endormi.

my Father protects his house
and her son.
This woman has done right
to leave without delay."

When he had said these words,
the Lord went to sit
on the old wooden bench
in front the old hut and, with a hand,
for a minute, spun the distaff
and rocked the little one.

Then getting up,
He signaled to Peter and left.
When she came back to her home,
the widow to whom in His kindness
God gave this proof, found
without ever guessing by which friend
her distaff spun and son fast asleep.

Phèdre (Pathé 1903)

G & T
Translated by Sheila Soman

Oui, Prince, je languis,
Je brule pour Thesee,
Je l'aime,
non point tel que l'ont vu les enfers,
Volage adorateur de mille objets divers
Qui va du Dieu des morts
deshonorer la couche;
Mais fidele, mais fier, et meme
un peu farouche,
Charmant, jeune, trainant tous les coeurs
après soi,
Tel qu'on depeint nos Dieux,
ou tel que je vous voi.

Il avait votre port, vos yeux,
votre langage,
Cette noble pudeur colorait son visage,
Lorsque de notre Crete il traversa les flots,
Digne sujet des voeux
des filles de Minos.

Yes, Prince, I languish,
I burn for Theseus,
I love him,
not as in the Underworld —
the ravager of a thousand women
who cuckolds even the
God of the dead;
But faithful, proud and
a little diffident;
Charming, young, trailing all the hearts
after him,
Such as they picture our Gods,
or such as I see you.

He has your carriage, your eyes,
your speech.
This noble shame reddens his face,
when he crossed the waves from Crete,
a worthy object of the vows
of Minos' daughters.

Sarah Bernhardt in *Phèdre*, one of the most difficult roles of her career. She made three recordings of passages from Racine's classic.

Que faisez-vous alors? Pourquoi,
sans Hippolyte,
des heros de la Grece assembla-t-il l'elite?
Pourquoi trop jeune encor ne putes-vous
Alors entrer dans le vaisseau
qui le mit sur nos bords?

What did you do then? Why then,
without Hippolyte,
the heros of Greece assemble the elite?
Why were you too young
to enter the vessels
that brought him to our shores?

Par vous aurait peri le
monster de la Crete
malgre tous les detours
de sa vaste retraite.
Pour en developer l'embarras incertain
Ma soeur du fil
fatal eut arme votre main.

You would have conquered the
monster of Crete
in spite of the many entanglements
of his vast domain.

My sister would have armed you
with the fatal thread.

Mais non,
dans ce dessein je l'aurais devancee.
L'Amour m'en eut d'abord inspire la pensee.

But no,
I would have proceeded.
Love first inspired my thoughts.

C'est moi, Prince, c'est moi,
dont l'utile secours vous eut
du Labyrinthe enseigne les detours.
Que de soins m'eut coutes cette tete
charmante!

Un fil n'eut point assez rassure
votre amante.
Compagne du peril
qu'il vous fallait chercher,
Moi-meme devant vous
j'aurais voulu marcher.
Et Phedre
au labyrinthe avec vous descendue,
Se serait avec vous retrouvee ou perdue.

It's me, Prince, it's me,
who gave you the necessary help
to learn the meshings of the Labyrinth.
How this has cost me dearly!

A simple thread would not have reassured
your lover.
But as a companion of your peril
to look for you,
myself before you,
I would have wanted to walk.
And your Phedre
to have descended the labyrinth,
to survive or perish with you.

La Mort d'Izail (The Death of Izail) (1903)

Written by Maurice Bernhardt; recorded in Paris
Translated by Alissa Webel

Izeil, Izeil était morte d'amour,
et fermés pour jamais à la clarté du jou,r
ses yeux s'étaient ouverts
sur l'aurore inconnue.

Izeil, Izeil had died of love,
and closed forever to the light of day,
her eyes had opened upon
an unknown dawn.

L'or du dernier couchant
caressait sa main nue,
et le simple linceul de sa robe,
aux plis droits s'allongeait
de son col langui avec effroi.

The gold of the last sunset
touching her naked hand,
and the simple shroud of her robe,
with strait folds stretched,
languished with fear, from her neck.

L'apôtre prirent son corps pudique et,
de leurs bras
au chant suprême du cantique,
que chantaient alentour les disciples pieux,
couchèrent le corps blanc
dans le berceau des dieux.

The apostles took her chaste body and,
in their arms,
to the supreme song of the canticle,
sung by the surrounding pious disciples,
laid the white body
in the cradle of the gods.

L'ombre, berceau des nuits,
d'où sort douce lumière,
alors, refleurissant dans sa vertu première,
jeune et vierge à nouveau,
belle et divinement pure,
et superbe ainsi qu'à son commencement,
par l'amour et par la douleur,
de soi laver Izeil.

The shadow, cradle of the night,
from which a soft light comes,
then blooming anew in her first virtue,
young and a virgin again,
beautiful and divinely pure,
and superb as at the beginning,
by love and by pain,
from her washed Izeil.

Ressurgit de la mort,	Birthed from death,
enlevée vers la vie,	lifted towards life
et monta sur l'air bleu	and ascended on the blue air
s'épanouir dans l'aube éternelle de Dieu.	to bloom in the eternal dawn of God.

Sarah originated the role of *Izéil* in 1894. Her son, Maurice Bernhardt, wrote this poem about Izéil, the girl who died of love, recorded by Sarah in 1903.

Théroigne de Méricourt's Dream
(Le Rêve de Théroigne de Méricourt) (1903)

Written by Paul Ernest Hervieu; recorded in Paris
Translated by Alissa Webel

Dans les profondeurs du sommeil,	In the depth of sleep,
j'entendais une immense acclamation.	I heard an immense cheer.
Une femme m'apparut.	A woman appeared to me.
De partout saillait ce même cri:	From everywhere jutted the same cry:
"Vive la Révolution!"	"Long live the Revolution!"
Mais dans les traits de son visage	But, in the traits of her face
je reconnus avec stupeur	I recognized with amazement
le mien.	my own.

C'était moi.	It was me.
J'incarnais la Révolution.	I embodied the Revolution.
J'étais parée de belles couleurs,	I was dressed with beautiful colors,
blanches, rouges et bleues.	white, red and blue.
Je tendais vers l'univers	I held out fraternal hands
des mains fraternelles.	to the universe.
Je prononçais des phrases sublimes.	I pronounced amazing speeches.
J'accomplissais des actes prodigieux.	I accomplished prodigious acts.
J'étais, vous dis-je, la Révolution!	I was, I tell you, the Revolution!
Soudain, le froid d'une bouche morte	Suddenly, the cold of a dead mouth
s'approcha de mon oreille.	approached my ear.
Et ce François	And this François
dont j'ai assuré l'immolation,	whose sacrifice I ensured,
me suivait et me disait:	followed me saying:
"Tu as goûté au moyen le plus	"You have tasted the surest way
sûr d'avoir toujours raison!	of always being right!
Tu ne te déshabitueras plus	You will never be able
de tuer le contradicteur,	to stop killing opponents,
de tuer pour qu'on cède,	killing for them to concede,
de tuer encore	killing again
parce que tu auras tué!"	because you will have killed!"
Et je me sentis précipiter	And I felt myself thrown
dans un sang pourpre.	into a crimson blood.
Sur l'autel roulaient	On the altar rolled
des milliers de têtes,	thousands of heads,
coupées, de toutes les [inaudible]:	cut heads, of all types:
têtes fines à cheveux d'argent,	fine heads with silver hair,
têtes halées d'où pendaient	tanned heads from which
des barbes grossières,	thick beards fell,
blondes têtes de femmes,	blond heads of women,
des têtes même d'enfants.	heads even of children.
Je me défendais contre	I fought against
leurs dents grinçantes, et je criais:	their grinding teeth and cried:
"Erreur! Erreur!	"Error! Error!
Vous me prenez pour la Tyrannie!	You mistake me for Tyranny!
Et c'est elle seule,	She alone,
qui depuis les origines du monde,	since the world's beginning,
a eu le loisir de faire tant	has had time to make
de têtes sans corps.	so many heads without bodies.
Moi, vous voyez	Me, don't you see
bien ma cocarde fraîche.	my brand new cockade!
Je suis la Liberté nouvelle!	I am the new Freedom!
Je suis la généreuse Révolution!"	I am the generous Revolution!"

Mais toutes les têtes au supplice
me répondaient:
"C'est pourtant toi!
C'est toi qui nous a tranché
au raz des épaules
ouvrant ainsi les sources rouges,
vidant les précieux réservoirs de sang
qui se sont perdus
dans cette mer immense."

"C'est toi! Toi!
Égale aux pires tyrannies!
Toi! Toi!
Révolution!"

But all the heads in agony
answered back:
"It is nevertheless you!
It is you who sliced our heads
down to our shoulders,
opening these red streams,
emptying precious reserves of blood
lost in this immense sea."

"It is you! You!
Equal to the worse tyrannies!
You! You!
Revolution!"

Sarah Bernhardt portrait ca. 1892 (from the collection of Peter van der Waal).

Sarah originated the role of *Théroigne de Méricourt* in 1902, recording the tortured tirade of Théroigne's dream in 1903.

Un Peu de Musique (Zonophone 1903)

By Victor Hugo
Translated by Sheila Soman

Si tu veux, faisons un rêve.	If you want, let us dream.
Montons sur deux palefrois.	Let us board two horses.
Tu m'emmènes, je t'enlève.	You take me, I carry you off.
L'oiseau chante dans les bois.	The bird sings in the woods.
Je suis ton maître et ta proie.	I am your master and your prey.
Partons, c'est la fin du jour.	Let us be off, it is end of day.
Mon cheval sera la joie,	My horse will be joy,
Ton cheval sera l'amour.	Your horse will be love.
Nous ferons toucher leurs têtes.	We will make their heads touch.
Les voyages sont aisés.	The trip will be easy.
Nous donnerons à ces bêtes	We will give these beasts
Une avoine de baisers.	Oats made of kisses.
Viens! nos doux chevaux mensonges	Come! Our two imaginary horses
Frappent du pied tous les deux.	Are both stomping their hooves.
Le mien, au fond de mes songes,	Mine, at the base of my dreams,
Et le tien au fond des cieux.	Yours at the base of the skies.
Un bagage est nécessaire.	Baggage is needed.
Nous emporterons nos vœux,	We will carry our vows,
Nos bonheurs, notre misère	Our happiness, our misery
Et la fleur de tes cheveux.	And a flower of your hair.
Viens, le soir brunit les chênes,	Come, the night is darkening the oaks,
Le moineau rit; ce moqueur,	The sparrow laughs, this mocker,
Entend le doux bruit des chaînes	He listens to the soft noise of the chains
Que tu m'as mises au cœur.	That you have placed on my heart.
Ce ne sera point ma faute	It will not be my fault
Si les forêts et les monts,	If the forests and mountains,
En nous voyant côte à côte,	Seeing us travel side by side,
Ne murmurent pas: Aimons!	Murmur "Let us love!"
Viens, sois tendre, je suis ivre.	Come, be kind, I am drunk.
Ô les verts taillis mouillés,	Oh the green, damp moss,
Ton souffle te fera suivre	Your breath will make them follow
Des papillons reveilles.	The awakened butterflies.

L'envieux oiseau nocturne,
Triste, ouvrira son œil rond.
Les nymphes, penchant leur urne
Dans les grottes, souriron.

The envious nocturnal bird,
Sad, will open his round eye.
The numphs, leaning over their urn
In the caves, will smile.

Et diront: "Sommes-nous folles!
C'est Léandre avec Héro,
En écoutant leurs paroles.
Nous laissons tomber notre eau.

And they will say "We are mad!"
It is Leandre with her Hero,
Listening to their words.
We let drop our water.

Allons-nous-en par l'Autriche!
Nous aurons l'aube à nos fronts;
Je serai grand, et toi riche,
Puisque nous nous aimerons.

Let us go through Austria.
We will have the dawn on our foreheads;
I will be great and you rich,
Then we will love.

Allons-nous-en par la terre,
Sur nos deux chevaux charmants,
Dans l'azur, dans le mystère
Dans les éblouissements.

Let us travel on earth
On our two charming horses,
Into the blue, into the mystery
Of the miracles.

Nous entrerons à l'auberge,
Et nous payerons l'hôtelier
De ton sourire de vierge
De mon bonjour d'écolier.

We will enter an inn
And we will pay the innkeeper
With your virgin smile
And my schoolboy joy.

Tu seras dame, et moi comte.
Viens, mon cœur s'épanouit.
Viens, nous conterons ce conte
Aux étoiles de la nuit.

You will be a lady and I a count.
Come, my heart is faint.
Come, let us tell our story
To the stars in the night.

Les Bouffons: La Brise Conte (The Breeze Tells) (1908)

Written by Miguel Zamaçois; recorded in Paris
Translated by Alissa Webel

Le souffle qui remue imperceptiblement,
cette jeune esprit
autour des yeux charmants
c'est l'âme d'un Zéphyr
dont je connais l'histoire
pour l'avoir déchiffré
un jour dans un couloir.

The breath which moves imperceptibly,
this young spirit
around charming eyes
is the soul of a Zephyr
whose story I know
for having deciphered it
one day in a corridor.

Donc, jadis, un Zéphyr,
planant, musant, rêvant,

So, a long time ago, a Zephyr,
hovering, dawdling, dreaming,

entra dans un très vieux castel
en coup de vent.

Et léger, il surgit,
frôla de son haleine
une enfant de seize ans
qui filait de la laine.

Ses yeux étaient du bleu
de ce lac resplendissant.
Dont il avait ridé la surface
en passant, lançant
pour rétablir la coquette harmonie,
de l'onduleux repli d'une boucle fournie.
Eut un geste du bras,
de la main et des doigts,
Si souple et si troublant,
et si chaste a la fois.

Que le petit zéphyr faiseur de pirouettes
qui contait ses amours
au son des girouettes
coutumier du mensonge
et gaspilleur d'aveux,
pour avoir vu passer
ses doigts dans ses cheveux,
senti qu'il n'aurait plus
désormais d'autre reine
que l'enfant de seize ans
qui filait de la laine.

Et dès lors,
la fillette entraîna sur ses pas
un amant qu'elle ne voyait pas.
Et lui tout heureux de pouvoir être encore
l'amoureux inconnue qui passe
et qu'on ignore,
dès qu'il apercevait
ses beaux yeux rembrunis
il courrait vite chercher des chansons
dans les nuits.

Ne pouvant apporter
toutes les fleurs dans l'herbe,
il a dû cueillir des papillons
dans l'herbe, des bois, des champs,
des jardins, et des bosquets.

entered a very old castle
in a gust of wind.

And light, there surged,
brushed with his breath
a sixteen year old child
spinning wool.

Her eyes were the blue
of that resplendent lake.
He had disturbed the surface
in passing, throwing,
in order to reestablish stylish harmony,
the sinuous wave of a full curl.
The gesture of her arm,
hand, fingers
was so supple, and so troubling,
and so chaste at the same time.

So the little pirouetting Zephyr
who told his loves
to the tune of weathervanes,
he, the customary liar
and vow squanderer,
for having seen her
run her fingers through her hair,
felt he could never again
have another for queen than
the sixteen year old child
spinning wool.

And, from then on,
in the girl's footsteps
followed a lover she didn't see.
And he, delighted to still be
the unknown lover who passes by
and is ignored,
as soon as he noticed
her darkened eyes
would run to gather songs
in the nights.

Unable to bring
all the flowers in the grass,
he had to pick butterflies
in the grass, forests, fields,
gardens, and groves.

Et quand il avait fait doucement
des bouquets de rubis,
palpitants de nacre, d'or et d'ambre,
son amour dans la chambre.

Au temps où se faisait aux prés la fenaison
allait chercher de quoi parfumer la maison
des senteurs de la sauge
ou de la marjolaine
pour l'enfant de seize ans
qui filait de la laine.

Parfois, jusqu'en Provence,
il allait voyager pour revenir
plus lourd de parfum d'oranger.

À chacun de ses maux
il trouvait un remède,
Et si la nuit était froide,
il rapportait arriva plus tiède.
Si l'air était brûlant
et le ciel orageux,
il rapportait du frais
des grands sommets neigeux.

Quand elle avait un livre,
effrontés comme un page,
il soufflait à propos
pour lui tourner sa page.

Puis, quand elle dormait
dans son petit dodo,
le Zéphyr doucement écartait le rideau,
y mêlait pour avoir
de son corps quelque chose
un souffle au souffle
pur de sa bouche mi-close.
Longtemps, il contemplait
l'harmonieux dessin des petits doigts
dormants sur la rondeur du sein,
et tout énamouré, pour apaiser ses fièvres
sans qu'elle eût à rougir,
la baisait sur les lèvres.

Hélas, un jour,
vêtu d'un somptueux pourpoint
un seigneur arriva que l'on ne connaissait
  point,

And when he had
softly made bouquets of ruby,
fluttering, shimmering gold and amber,
his love in the room.

When in the fields it was hay-time,
would seek out that to perfume the house
with scents of salvia
and sweet marjoram
for the sixteen year old child
spinning wool.

Sometimes all the way to Provence,
he would travel to return
filled with orange blossom scents.

To all her ails
he found remedy,
and, if the night was cold,
he would arrive warmer.
If the air was burning,
and the sky stormy,
he would bring back fresh air
from the snowy mountain tops.

When she had a book,
shameless as a pageboy,
he would blow in perfect time
to turn her page.

Then, as she slept
in her little bed,
the Zephyr gently opened her curtain
and mingled there,
to have of her body a thing,
a breath to her pure breath
from her half-closed mouth.
A while, he would contemplate
the harmonious design of small fingers
sleeping on the curves of her breast,
and all enamored, to appease his fevers
without need for her to blush,
would kiss her lips.

Alas, one day,
dressed in a sumptuous doublet
arrived an unknown lord.

Il était jeune et fier,
il venait d'Aquitaine
pour épouser l'enfant qui filait de la laine.

Young and proud,
he came from Aquitaine
to marry the child spinning wool.

Ah, si sa beauté, quelques riches présents
sans peine eurent raison
de ce coeur de seize ans.
Après le grand salut
et des compliments vagues,
on parla mariage,
on échangea des bagues.

Ah, if his looks and after rich gifts
won without trouble this heart
sixteen years of age.
After the great introduction
and some vague compliments,
talk was made of marriage,
rings exchanged.

Aussi parfumés qu'ils soient,
que peuvent les Zéphyrs
contre les cavaliers qui donnent des saphirs,
des perles et des colliers.

As perfumed as they may be,
what can Zephyrs do
against knights giving sapphires,
pearls, and necklaces.

Un souffle de tempête
le zéphyr a soufflé le castel en tête.
Pendant des jours des nuits,
on l'entendit hurler
toquant les vieux murs
pour les faire écrouler.

A storming gale,
the Zephyr blew against the castle.
Days and nights,
its cries were heard
hitting the old walls
to make them tumble.

Et le jour
ou l'on fût en cortège à l'église,
tour à tour orage ou bise,
pour qu'on en chemin
par monceaux il effeuilla
d'un coup les roses des berceaux.

And the day
when the procession went to church
blistering storms turned,
so that on the way, by heaps,
he stripped at once
the roses from the carriages.

Enfin, suprême espoir,
pendant le Saint Office
iIl tenta de sécher le vin
dans le calice,
et malgré les efforts du vieux sonneur,
très las,
força la grosse cloche
à ne sonner qu'un glas.

Lastly, ultimate hope,
during the Holy Mass
he attempted to dry the wine
in the chalice,
and despite all the old bell-ringer's
efforts, very tired,
forced the big bell
to ring only once.

Left: Sarah Bernhardt originated the role of Jacasse in *Les Bouffon* in 1907. A whimsical poem from the play, about a love-struck zephyr enraptured with a girl spinning wool, charmed the public on her 1908 recording. *Right:* In 1900 Sarah Bernhardt burst upon the theatrical world with her sensational performance as the Duc de Reichstadt in *L'Aiglon.* In 1910 she made what is possibly her most dramatic recording, a long scene from the play featuring a number of other actors.

L'Aiglon Act V, Scene V (Edison 1910)

Translated by Sheila Soman

Le Duc:	Duke:
Flambeau!	Flambeau!
Mais ce soldat couche la, maintenant,	That soldier, lying there now,
me fait peur!	frightens me!
Eh bien! Quoi! Ca n'a rien d'etonnant	Ah, well. It's nothing astonishing
qu'un grenadier francais dans cette herbe	that a French grenadier is asleep
s'endorme,	on the grass.
Et cette herbe connait deja cet uniforme!	And this grass knows well this uniform!
(Il se penche sur Flambeau, en lui criant)	(He leans over Flambeau, crying to him)
Oui, la victoire!	Yes, victory!
Au bout des fusils, les shakos!	Put down your guns, your shakos!

Des Voix, dans le vent:	Voices, in the wind:
A boire!... A boire!...	Water!... Water!...

Le Duc:
(tressaillant)
Oh!— Quels sont ces echos?

Duke:
(trembling)
Oh!— What are these cries?

Des Voix:
Je meurs… Je meurs…

Voices:
I'm dying… I'm dying

Le Duc:
(avec epouvante)
Son rale Se multiplie au loin…

Duke:
(with trembling)
It's cry is growing in the distance…

Une Voix:
(se perdant)
Je meurs…

A Voice:
(fading)
I'm dying…

Le Duc:
…sous le ciel pale!…
— Ah! Je comprends!… Le cri de
cet homme qui meurt,
fut pour ce val qui sait
tous les rales par coeur,
comme le premier vers
d'une chanson connue,
Et quand l'homme se tait,
la plaine continue!

Duke:
…under the pale sky!…
Ah! I see!…It is the cry of
this man who is dying,
made for this valley that knows
all the cries by heart,
as the first verse of
a well-known song,
and when the man falls silent,
the plain continues!

La Plaine, au loin:
Ah!… Ah!…

The Plain, in the distance:
Ah!… Ah!…

Le Duc:
Ah! Je comprends!… plainte, rale, sanglot,
C'est Wagram, maintenant, qui se
   souvient tout haut!

Duke:
Ah! I understand… this cry, rale, sob,
It's now Wagram that is calling out loud!

La Plaine, longuement:
Ah!…

The Plain, lengthily:
Ah!…

Le Duc:
(regardant Flambeau
qui s'est raidi dans l'herbe)

Il ne bouge plus!

(Avec terreur)

Il faut que je m'en aille!
Il a vraiment trop l'air tue dans la bataille!…

Duke:
(looking at Flambeau,
stretched out on the grass)

He's not moving!

(With terror)

I want to leave!
He looks too much as someone dead in
   battle…

(Sans le quitter des yeux,
il s'eloigne a reculons, en murmurant)

Ce devait etre tout a fait comme cela!
Cet habit bleu... ce sang...

(Et tout d'un coup il prend la fuite,
mais il s'arrete, comme si le soldat mort
etait encore devant lui)

Un autre...

(Il veut s'enfuir d'un autre cote,
mais il recule encore en criant)

Un autre, la!...

(Une troisieme fois il est arrete)

La...

(Il regarde autour de lui)

Partout, s'allongeant, les memes formes
bleues... Il en meurt!...

(Reculant toujours comme devant
un flot qui monte, il s'est refugie
au sommet du tertre
d'ou il decouvre toute la plaine)

Il en meurt ainsi pendant des lieues!...

Tout la Plaine:
Je meurs... Je meurs... Je meurs...

Le Duc:
Et que disent-ils, dans cette ombre, en rampant?

Une Voix, dans les hautes herbes:
Mon front saigne!

Une Autre:
Ma jambe est morte!

Une Autre:
Mon bras pend!

Le Duc:
Ah! Des buissons de bras se crispent sur la plaine!

(Without lifting his eyes,
he moves away, murmuring)

That is what it must look like!
This blue suit... this blood...

(Suddenly, he takes flight,
but stops as if the dead soldier
is still in front of him)

Another...

(He goes to run the other way
but stops again crying)

Another... There...

(A third time, he is stopped)

There...

(He looks around him)

They're all around... the same blue
forms... They are dying...

(Recoiling again before the
mounting masses, he escapes
to the top of the barrow
where he sees the entire plain)

They are dying for miles...

The Entire Plain:
I'm dying... I'm dying... I'm dying...

Duke:
And what do they cry out from these shadows?

A Voice, in the high grass:
My forehead bleeds!

Another:
My leg is dead!

Another:
My arm is hanging!

The Duke:
Ah! Groves of arms are cracking in the plain!

(Il veut marcher)	(He wants to walk)
Et je foule un gazon d'epaulettes de laine!	I've just touched a lawn of epaulettes!

Un Cri, a droite:	**A Cry, to the right:**
A moi!	Help me!

Le Duc:	**The Duke:**
(chancelant)	(shivering)
J'ai glisse sur un baudrier du cuir!...	I've just slipped on a leather belt!
(Il va vers la gauche, faisant a chaque instant le mouvement d'enjamber)	(He goes to the left, at each step almost tripping)

Un Voix, a gauche:	**A Voice, to the left:**
Dragon! Tends-moi les mains!	Dragoon! Give me your hands!

Une Autre:	**Another:**
(repondant froidement)	(replying coldly)
Je n'en ai plus.	I no longer have any.

Le Duc:	**The Duke:**
(eperdu)	(lost)
Ou fuit?	There's nowhere to go.
Il en meurt dans les pres,	They are dying in the fields,
dans les bles, dans les herbes.	in the weeds, in the grass...

Une Voix:	**A Voice:**
A boire!...	Water!

Le Duc:	**Duke:**
Hélas! Où sont les aigles?	Alas! Where are the eagles?
Ah! Je comprends pourquoi la nuit je me reveille!...	Ah! I understand why I wake at night!...
Pourquoi d'horribles toux	Why those horrible coughs
me mettent en sueurs!	send me into sweats!
Et je sais ce que c'est que le sang que je crache!	And I understand the blood that I spit!

Toute La Plaine:	**The Entire Plain:**
(hurlant de douleur)	(screaming from pain)
Ah!... Ah!...	Ah!... Ah!...

Le Duc:	**Duke:**
Et tous ces bras!	And all these arms!
Tous ces bras que je vois!	All these arms before me!
Tous ces poignets sans mains,	All these wrists without hands,
toutes ces mains sans doigts!	all these hands without fingers!

Monstrueuse moisson qu'un large vent	Monstrous moss as a large wind
qui passé semble coucher vers moi	that passes seems to settle near
pour me maudire!…	so to curse me!…
Grace! Ne me regardez pas avec ces yeux!	Don't look at me with those eyes!
Pourquoi?	Why?
Rampez-vous, tout d'un coup, en silence,	Why do you break this silence suddenly
vers moi?	towards me?
Dieu!	Gods!
Vous voulez crier quelque chose, il me	Why do you seem to cry out like this?
semble!…	
Pourquoi reprenez-vous haleine tous	Why do you hold your breath as one?
ensembler?	
Et courbe par l'epouvante, voulant fuir, ne	Why do you open your mouths filled with
pas entendre.	horror?
	And cringing in fright, wanting to flee,
	but not daring.
Quoi? Qu'allez-vous crier? Quoi?	What? What do you want to say? What?

Toutes Les Voix:	**All the Voices:**
Vive l'Empereur!	Long live the Emperor!

Phèdre (Act II, Scene V) (Edison 1910)

Translated by Sheila Soman

Phèdre:	**Phèdre:**
Oui, Prince, je languis,	Yes, Prince, I languish,
je brule pour Thesee,	I burn for Theseus,
Je l'aime, non point tel que l'ont vu	I love him, not as in
les enfers,	the Underworld —
voltage adorateur de mille objets divers,	the ravager of a thousand women,
qui va du die des morts deshonorer la couche;	who cuckolds even the god of the dead;
Mais fidele, mais fier, et meme	But faithful, proud, and
un peu farouche,	a little diffident;
Charmant, jeune, trainant tous les coeurs	Charming, young, trailing all the hearts
après soi,	after him,
Tel qu'on depeint nos adieux,	Such as they picture our gods,
ou tel que je vous voi.	or such as I see you.
Il avait votre port, vos yeux, votre langage,	He has your carriage, your eyes, your speech,
Cette noble pudeur colorait son visage,	This noble shame reddens his face,
Lorsque de notre Crete il traversa les flots,	when he crossed the waves from Crete,
dine sujet des voeux des filles de Minos.	a worthy object of the vows of Minos'
	daughters.

Above: The famous photograph of Sarah Bernhardt's tears, widely circulated around the world on postcards (from the collection of Peter van der Waal). *Right:* Sarah Bernhardt in the title role of *Phèdre*, the classic drama by Racine.

Que faisez-vous alors?
Pourquoi sans Hippolyte
des heros de la Grece assembla-t-il l'elite?
Pourquoi trop jeune
encor ne putes-vous alors
entrer dans le vaisseau qui le mit
sur nos bords?

Par vous aurait peri
le monster de la Crete
malgre tous les detours
de sa vaste retraite.
Pour en developer l'embarras incertain
Ma soeur du fil fatal eut arme votre main.

Mais non,
dans ce dessein je l'aurais devancee.

L'Amour m'en eut d'abord inspire la pensee.

What did you do then?
Why then, without Hippolyte,
the heros of Greece assemble the elite?
Why were you too young
to enter the vessels that brought him
to our shores?

You would have conquered
the monster of Crete
in spite of the many entanglements
of his vast domain.
My sister would have armed you
with the fatal thread.

But no,
I would have proceeded.

Love first inspired my thoughts.

C'est moi, Prince, c'est moi,
dont l'utile secours vous eut
du Labyrinthe enseigne les detours.
Que de soins m'eut coutes cette tete charmante!

Un fil n'eut point
assez rassure votre amante.
Compagne du peril qu'il vous fallait
chercher,
Moi-meme devant vous j'aurais voulu
marcher.

Et Phedre,
au labyrinthe avec vous descendue,
se serait avec vous retrouvee ou perdue.

Hippolyte:

Dieux! Quest-ce que j'entends?
Madame, oubliez-vous
que Thesee est mon pere,
et qu'il est votre epoux?

Phèdre:

Et sur quoi jugez-vous
que j'en perds la memoire, Prince?
Aurais-je perdu tout le soin
de ma gloire?

Hippolyte:

Madame, pardonnez.
J'avoue en rougissant,
Que j'accusaid a tort un discours innocent.
Ma honte ne peut plus
soutenir votre vue, Et je vais...

Phèdre:

Ah! Cruel, tu m'as trop
entendue.
Je t'en ai dit assez pour te tirer d'errèur.
Et bien, connais donc
Phedre, et toute sa fureur, J'aime.
Ne pense pas qu'au moment
que je t'aime innocente
a mes yeux je m'approuve moi-meme,
Ni que du fol amour qui trouble ma raison.
Ma lache complaisance ait nourri le poison.

It's me, Prince, it's me,
who gave you the necessary help
to learn the meshings of the Labyrinth.
How this has cost me dearly!

A simple thread
would not have reassured your lover.
But as a companion of your peril
to look for you,
Myself before you I would have
wanted to walk.

And your Phedre,
to have descended the labyrinth,
to survive or perish with you.

Hippolyte:

Oh, Gods! What is it I hear?
Madame, are you forgetting
that Theseus is my father
and your husband?

Phèdre:

And do you believe
I've lost my memory, Prince?
And that I've lost all attention
to my glory?

Hippolyte:

Madame, forgive me.
I admit in blushing that I misunderstood
what you said.
My shame forbids me from
looking at you, I must go...

Phèdre:

Oh cruelty! You torture me
beyond endurance.
I have said enough to remove any doubt.
Now, know for a fact that
Phedre, in all her ardour, loves.
But don't think for a moment
that I consider Myself innocent
in my love for you,
That my mad love disturbs my reason.
My cowardly compliance
has nourished this poison.

Objet infortune des vengeances celestes,   Wretched object of divine vengence.
Je m'abhorre encor plus que   I hate myself more than
tu me detestes.   your hatred for me.
Les dieux m'en sont temoins,   The gods are my witness,
ces dieux qui dans mon flanc ont allume   those same gods who have lit me
le feu fatal a tout mon sang.   with horrible flames fatal to my blood.
Ces dieux qui se sont fait une gloire   Those gods have made a cruel glory
cruelle de seduire le coeur   in seducing the heart
d'ume faible mortelle.   of a weak mortal.

Toi-meme en ton esprit rappel le passé.   You yourself remember what happened.
C'est peu de t'avoir fui cruel,   I was cruel to shun you,
je t'ai chasse.   to have you chased.

J'ai voulu te paraitre odieuse, inhumaine.   I wanted to seem to you hateful, inhumane.
Pour mieux te resister,   In order to better resist you —
j'ai recherché ta haine.   I wanted you to hate me.

De quoi m'ont profite   And what has come of
mes inutiles soins?   these useless endeavors?
Tu me haissaid plus,   You hate me more,
je ne t'aimais pas moins.   I do not love you any less.
Test malheurs te pretaient encore   Your misfortunes cause you
de nouveaux charmes.   to take on more charms.
J'ai langui, j'ai seche, dans les feux,   I have languished, consumed in the fires,
dans les larmes.   in the tears.

Il suffit de tes yeux pout t'en persuader.   All it took were your eyes to persuade me.
Si tes yeux un moment   If your eyes were only to look at me
pouvaient me regarder.   for one moment.

Que dis-je? Cet aveu que je te viens de faire,   What do I say? This confession that I just made,
Cet aveu si honteux, le crois-tu volontaire?   this shameful confession,
Tremblante pour un fils que je n'osais trahir.   do you believe it voluntary?

Je te venais prier de ne le point hair.   Trembling for a son that I dare not deceive.
Faibles projets d'un coeur trop   I have come to beg you
plein de ce qu'il aime!   not to hate the weak plans
                                                 of a heart so full of love!

Helas! Je ne t'ai pu parler que de toi-meme.   Alas, I can no longer speak just of you.
Venge-toi!   Avenge yourself!
Punis-moi d'un odieux amour.   Punish me for this odious love,
Digne fils du heros qui t'a donne le jour.   O worthy hero — she who gave you life.
Delivre l'univers   Deliver the universe of this
d'un monster qui t'irrite.   monster of yours.

La veuve de Thesee ose aimer Hipployte!
Crois-moi, ce monster affreux ne doit
point t'echapper.
Voila mon Coeur.
C'est la que ta main doit frapper.
Impatient deja d'expier son offense.
Au-devant de ton bras je le sens qui s'avance.
Frappe.

Ou si tu le crois indigne de tes coups,
Si ta haine m'envie un supplice si doux,
Ou si d'un sang trop vil ta main serait
    trempee.
Au defaut de ton bras,
prete-moi ton eppe. Donne!

Theseus' widow dares to love Hippolyte!
Trust that this monster
doesn't escape you.
Here is my heart.
It is there that you must strike.
Hesitant to carry out its offense.
Over your arm, I feel its approach.
Stike.

Or, if you believe yourself
unworthy of these blows,
if your hate causes such sweet torture,
Or, if you hesitate
at the blood on your hands,
instead of by your hands,
give me your sword. Give!

La Samaritaine (Act I, Scene V) (Edison 1910)

Translated by Sheila Soman

Photine:
(Elle est arrive au puits, et,
sans regarder Jesus, elle attache l'urne
a la corde; elle la laisse lentement
descendre dans le puits.)

Photine:
(She arrives at the well and,
without noticing Jesus, she attaches
her pitcher to the rope and
lowers it slowly into the well.)

Je dormais. Quelquefois je dors,
mais tout de meme mon Coeur veille.
Quelqu'un m'a crie du dehors:
"Ouvrez, coeur, fleur, aster,
merveille!"

I was sleeping. Sometimes, I sleep,
but all the same, my heart keeps guard.
Someone called from outside:
"Open, my heart, my flower, my star,
my marvel!"

J'ai repondu d'un ton malin
A la chere voix reconnue:
"J'ai quitte ma robe de lin:
Puis-je vous ouvrir? Je suis nue.

I replied in an irritated tone
To the voice I knew so well:
I've taken off my linen robe:
You want me to open? I am nude.

J'ai parfume mes pieds laves
prealablement dans la neige:
Mes pieds blancs, sur les noirs paves,
Pour vous ouvrir, les salirai-je."

I bathed and perfumed my feet
carefully in the snow:
My white feet on the dark ground.
To open for you, I would get them dirty.

Je dis... Mais je fus vite ourvrir:
Contre lui je suis si peu forte!
Il avait fui: j'ai cru mourir,
Et quand j'eus referme la porte

I said... But still I quickly opened:
I am so weak to his will!
He had fled; I nearly died.
And when I closed the door

(Mes doigts avaient sur les verrous   (My fingers had left on the lock
laisse de la myrrhe sauvage),   a trace of wild myrrh)
J'ai pleure dans mes cheveux roux   I wept into my red hair
et me suis griffe le visage.   and slapped myself on the face.

Jesus:

Pas un instant sur moi ne s'est fixe son oeil.   She hasn't noticed me for an instant.

Photine:

Faira-t-il devant moi, toujours,   Will he flee at the site of me,
comme un cheuvreuil?   as a phantom?

Jesus:

Voici qu'elle commence a remonter l'amphore.   Here she is pulling the pitcher up.

Photine:

(Tournant la it de bois qui tire la corde.)   (Turning the wheel that pulls the cord.)

Mon bien-aime — je t'ai cherche —   My beloved — I have searched for you —
depuis l'aurore,   ever since dawn,
Sans le trouver, — et it u trouve —   In vain — now I find you again —
et c'est le soir;   and it is night;
Mais it u bonheur! — il ne fait pas —   But what chance! — It's not —
tout a fait nori: it's not quite dark;
Mes yeux encore pourront te voir.   My eyes still will be able to see you.

Ton nom repand — toutes les huiles —   Your name comes back — all the oils —
principales ton soufflé unit —   the main ones your breath unites —
tous les parfums — essentials,   all the perfumes — the essentials,
Tes moindre mots — sont composes —   Your smallest words — are composed —
de tous les miels,   of honey,
Et tes yeux pales de tous les it u.   And your pale eyes are from above.

Mon it u se fond — comme un fruit tender —   My heart is empty — as a tender fruit —
et sans ecorce...   and without hope...
Oh! Sur ce it u, — mon bien-aime —   Oh! On your heart — my beloved —
qui te cherchait!   how I searched.
Viens te poser — avec douceur —   Come to me — sweetly —
comme un sachet,   as a sachet,
Puis avec force comme un cachet!   Then with force as a seal!

Jesus:

Dans le rond de l'amphore pleine elle se   In the mouth of the pitcher she admires her-
mire...   self...

Photine:

Comme un cachet d'airain, comme un sachet de myrrhe!...

Jesus:

Femme!

> (Elle se retourne et le regarde
> d'un air insolent.)

J'ai soif; car les rayons du soleil sont tres vifs.
Fais-moi boire, veux-tu!

Photine:

Je croyais que les Juifs —
et cet it en est un —
cela se connait vite —
ne pouvaient pas avec quiconque est Sichemite,
avoir le plus leger, le plus lointain rapport!

Notre pain, c'est pour eux de la viande de porc;
Un it, l a Sichem l'abeille aurait sa ruche,
Serait du sang d'oiseau pour eux!
Donc, cette cruche qui, toute fraiche,
sort d'un puits Samaritain,
et que, sur son front vil,
une paienne tint,
tu devrais l'ecarter d'un geste execratoire,
au lieu de demander...

Jesus:

It u demande a boire.

Photine:

Ton degout par la soif est donc diminue?
Sache que tu serais beaucoup moins
Pollue en foulant un reptile, en touchant
un insecte, qu'en etant secouru par
   quelqu'un de ma secte!

> (Avec une volubilite mechante)

Non, quand tu m'en prirais it u jusqu'a demain,
it u descendrai pas la cruche sur ma main:
Elle est sur mon epaule; elle est bien;
je l'emporte.

Adieu, l'Eliezer sans cadeaux,
sans escorte!

Photine:

As a seal of brass, as a sachet of myrrh...

Jesus:

Woman!

> (She turns around and looks at him
> with insolence.)

I'm thirsty; the rays of the sun are strong.
Give me something to drink!

Photine:

I believe that Jews —
and this man is one —
you can see right away —
cannot have with any Sichemite,
the lightest, or the most distant relation!

Our bread, for them, is pork;
Honey, of which the Sichem bee has its hive,
Will be the blood of a bird for them!
So, this pitcher, which is freshly filled
from a Samaritain well,
and which, on his evil forehead,
a tinged place,
you must refuse with a careless gesture
instead of demanding...

Jesus:

I ask for a drink.

Photine:

Your disgust is diminished by your thirst?
Know that you will be less disgusted
by touching a reptile or an insect
than in seeking help from one of my sect!

> (With increasing anger)

No, you can beg all night long,
I will not let you touch my pitcher.
It is on my shoulder, it goes well there,
I will not take it down.

Farewell, Elizer without gifts,
without escort!

It u me pris pour Rebecca,
tu te trompas!
Tu dois avoir bien soif!
Mais tu ne boiras pas.

      (Redescendant un peu)

Tu vois cette eau,
cette eau limpide, si limpide que lorsqu'il
   en est plein,
le vase semble vide,
Si fraiche que l'on voit en larmes de lueur,
en perles de claret ruisseler la sueur,
La sueur de fraicheur que l'amphor pansue,
Par tous les pores fins de son argile, sue!
Cette eau qui donne soif rien,
qu'avec son bruit clair,
si legere qu'elle est comme
une liqueur d'air,
Eh bien! Pour toi, cette eau, c'est la loi,
la loi dure,
Cette eau pure, cette eau si pure,
elle est impure!

If you take me for Rebecca,
you are mistaken!
You deserve to be thirsty!
I will not give you to drink.

      (Returning a bit)

You see this water,
this water that is oh so clear,

that when the pitcher is full,
it seems empty,
So fresh that tears that fall
seems like pearls in comparison.
The sweat of the filled pitcher,
through all its pores perspires!
This water that causes thirst,
with it's gentle sound
so light that it is almost like liquid air.
Oh well! For you, this water, it is the law,
and the law endures.
This water, this pure water,
is impure!

In 1910 Sarah Bernhardt made a longer, four-minute recording of her role as Photine, the woman at the well, in *La Samaritaine*. The longer recording time offered the opportunity to bring into the recorded performance another actor as Jesus.

L'Etoile dans la Nuit
(The Star in the Night) (1918)

Written by Emile Guerinon and Henri Cain
Translated by Alissa Webel

Oh! Toi, dont j'ai gardé
la vision divine
telle qu'elle s'offrit
au jour plus loin de nous
où ton dernier regard
qui enfin m'illumine.

Oh! You, of whom I have kept
the divine vision
as she appeared
in the far gone day of us
when your last gaze
enlightening me now, at last.

Toi, que je vois toujours
radieuse et frêle.
Toi que chante à jamais
mon souvenir pieu.

You, that I always see
radiant and frail.
You for whom forever sings
my pious memory.

Toi, mon ultime matin,
mon poème, ma reine,
ma grande amie!
Oh, toi, ma femme devant Dieu.

You, my ultimate morning,
my poem, my queen,
my great friend !
Oh, you, my wife in front of God.

Pardonne-moi
d'avoir le triste courage
de t'écarter ma main de la tienne,
et d'oser Arrêter notre livre
à l'endroit de la page
où le doigt du malheur
sur mon nom s'est posé.

Forgive me
for having the sad courage
of removing my hand from yours,
for daring to stop our book
at the precise place on the page
where the finger of sadness
fell on my name.

Dans ma prison d'oubli,
de nuit et de silence,
tu ne descendras pas
car à l'amour
il faut le soleil éclatant,
il faut des sentiments
pour vivre et pour voler plus haut,
toujours plus haut.

In my prison of forgetfulness,
night and silence
you will not descend to,
because with love
must come bright sun;
it must have feelings
to live and fly higher,
always higher.

Puis, sur l'attente qu'on les destinait
triste des clairs bonheurs
que je rêvais pour toi,
ne jamais soupçonner dans leur
vol des années que tu restes
toujours au temple de ma foi.

Then, on the expectations we held
for them, sad of the clear happiness
I dreamt for you,
never suspect in their flight,
over years that you remain
always in the temple of my faith.

Que tu as placé le socle de lumière	That you placed the pedestal of light
Vers d'immenses d'adoration,	towards immense adoration,
Je serai toujours là devant toi,	I will always be there seeing you,
droite et fière,	strait and proud before me,
mirages débilitants,	debilitating delusions,
splendides visions.	splendid visions.
Qui inventent l'amour	Who invents love
à la minute dernière,	at the last minute,
miraculeusement belle d'émotions.	miraculously beautiful with emotions.
Puisses-tu, de ton ciel	May you, joyful in your sky
ou je te veux joyeuse,	where I want you,
Te savoir aimée.	know yourself loved.
Oh pure étoile de la nuit !	Oh pure star in the night!

Prière pour Nos Ennemis
(A Prayer for our Enemies) (1918)

Translated by Alissa Webel

Vous qui récompensez	O Thou who rewards,
dit-on, le sacrifice,	they say, sacrifice,
vous qui savez peser	Thou who knowest to weigh
et juger l'idéal	and judge the ideal
dont un peuple se fait	of which a people offers itself
le lige et le féal,	the servant and liege,
Vous qui ne voulez pas	Thou who allowest not
que l'innocent pâtisse,	that the innocent suffer,
Vous devant qui l'orgueil du mal	Thou before whom the pride of evil
n'est pas permis, lorsque pour nous,	cannot stand, when, for us,
ainsi que pour nos ennemis,	as well as for our enemies,
nous entendrons sonner	the hour of judgment shall strike,
l'heure de la justice,	
Vous qui voyez, Seigneur,	O Lord, thou who seest
leur âme jusqu'au fond,	into the depths of their souls,
ne leur pardonnez pas,	do not forgive them
ils savent ce qu'ils font.	for they know what they do.
Ils ont souillé de sang	They smeared with blood
les pages de l'histoire,	the pages of history,
trahissant les serments,	betraying their oaths,
déchirant les traités;	tearing up treaties;

Du Théâtre au Champ d'Honneur featured Sarah in 1916 as Marc, an unknown soldier, struggling to recover from a bombardment. A patriotic speech from this play, titled *A Prayer for Our Enemies*, was Sarah's choice for her final recording in 1918.

Ils ont fait reculer d'un bond l'humanité
jusqu'au seuil oublié des heures
les plus noires.

They have pushed mankind back a stroke
as far as the forgotten threshold
of the darkest times.

Et lorsque devant eux,
dans un suprême effort,
un people au déshonneur
a préféré la mort,
ils l'ont, sans frémir,
crucifié dans sa gloire.

And when, facing them
in a sublime effort,
a people preferred death to dishonor,
they crucified it in its glory,
without a pang of remorse.

Vous qui voyez, Seigneur,
leur âme jusqu'au fond
ne leur pardonnez pas,
ils savent ce qu'ils font.

O Lord, Thou who seest
into the depths of their souls,
do not forgive them
for they know what they do.

Quand, du pulpe du mal,
renouvelant les rites
du soldat ils font des assassins
funèbre dessein
s'abat sur les cités,
quand par eux sont proscrites
toutes les infamies, toutes les cruautés.

When, from the flesh of evil,
renewing the rites
of the soldier, they make assassins
morbid design
befall the cities,
when by them are banished
all ignominies, all inhumanities.

S'il est vrai contre ses amours
et de bontés de tout être
qui va Vous user, démérite,

Vous qui voyez, Seigneur,
leur âme jusqu'au fond
ne leur pardonnez pas,
ils savent ce qu'ils font.

Ô Vous qu'ils ont osé
vouloir mettre à leur tête,
Vous qu'ils osent
encore invoquer sans trembler,
Seigneur, dans votre jour
qui bientôt va briller,
de toutes parts sur
eux déchaînez la tempête.
Et s'ils se repentent,
dédaignez leur repentir.
Que vos bontés pour eux
refusent de fleurir.
Donnez des lendemains
sans nombre à leur défaite!

Vous qui voyez, Seigneur,
leur âme jusqu'au fond,
ne leur pardonnez pas,
ils savent ce qu'ils font.

Qu'ils souffrent de la faim,
que leur soit révélée
dans leur âme et leur chair
la loi du talion.

Que le coeur plein
de haine et de rébellion,
ils voient de leur pays toute paix exilée.

Qu'un jour, par des guerriers,
nouveaux fils de la nuit,
comme ils l'ont fait chez nous,
leurs temples soient détruits,
leurs enfants mutilés
et leurs femmes violées.

Vous qui voyez, Seigneur,
leur âme jusqu'au fond,

If it is true that against their loves
and benevolence
any being who uses You, demerits.

O Lord, thou who seest into
the depths of their souls,
do not forgive them
for they know what they do.

Thou whom they still dare
to call as leader,
Thou whom they still dare
to invoke without trembling,
Lord, in thy day which is soon to break,
unleash everywhere against them
the storm.
If they repent, scorn their repentance.
May thy love
refuse to unfold itself for them.
Give to their defeat
an endless aftermath!

O Lord, thou who seest
into the depths of their souls,
do not forgive them
for they know what they do.

May they suffer hunger,
may they see revealed
in their soul and their flesh
the full retaliation.

May they,
with hearts full of hatred and revolt,
see peace exiled from their land.

May, one day, warriors,
new sons of the night,
their temples be destroyed,
as they have done unto us,
their children maimed
and wives raped.

O Lord, thou who seest
into the depths of their souls,

ne leur pardonnez pas,	do not forgive them
ils savent ce qu'ils font.	for they know what they do.
Abreuvez-les de pleurs.	Overwhelm them with tears.
Faites que rien n'efface	Let nothing ever cleanse
l'horreur du crime	the horror of the crime
dont palpite l'univers;	which makes the world shudder;
Doublez pour eux	Double for them
les maux dont nous avons souffert.	the suffering we have suffered.
Frappez-les, ô Seigneur,	Smite them, O Lord,
d'une main jamais lasse,	with a hand never weary,
jusqu'au jour où, pour délivrer l'humanité,	till the day when, to deliver mankind,
Votre juste vengeance,	Thy just vengeance,
en sa sure équité,	in its infallible equity,
du monde pour jamais	from the Earth forever
abolira leur race.	shall abolish their race.
Vous qui voyez, Seigneur,	O Lord, thou who seest
leur âme jusqu'au fond,	into the depths of their souls,
ne leur pardonnez pas,	do not forgive them
ils savant ce qu'ils font.	for they know what they do.

Part 3
FILMS

Introduction

Year	Original Title	Alternative Title
1900	Le Duel d'Hamlet	Hamlet
1908	La Tosca	Tosca
1911	La Dame aux Camélias	Camille
1912	Sarah Bernhardt à Belle Isle	Sarah Bernhardt at Home
1912	Les Amours de la Reine Elisabeth	Queen Elizabeth
1913	Adrienne Lecouvreur	An Actress's Romance
1915	Ceux de Chez Nous	Those at Our House
1915	Jeanne Doré	
1917	Mères Françaises	Mothers of France
1919	It Happened in Paris	
1921	Daniel	
1923	La Voyante	The Fortune Teller

From the inception of motion pictures, various inventors attempted to unite sight and sound through "talking" motion pictures. In the fall of 1895 the Edison Company experimented with this in a film known today as *Dickson Experimental Sound Film*. As two men dance, the film shows a man playing a violin. The film has survived, but for a century the sound disc had been lost. In 2001 the wax cylinder with the matching sound recording was discovered and restored to the film, marrying image and sound into a whole, as was planned with the original experiment.

In 1895 Edison was providing Kineto-phones for viewers to view motion pictures and sound in synchronous action. The Kinetophone was a combined Kinetoscope motion picture machine and phonograph inside a single cabinet. Peepholes were built through which a viewer could watch the projected image, while two rubber ear tubes provided a way to listen to the accompanying phonograph. The machine drew initial attention to the novelty but soon separated into two devices for the consumption of the masses.

During the great Paris Exposition of 1900, at the age of 56, Sarah made her film debut. She filmed the brief duel scene from

Sarah Bernhardt and Coquelin Aine, who both starred in one of the first sound-on-film experiments in the Phono-Film Exhibit at the Paris Exposition of 1900.

Hamlet, more as a technological experiment than a work of art. The motion picture was part of a program devised by Mme. Marguerite Chenu for the first talkie theater, the Phono-Cinema-Theatre. This was Mme. Chanu's enterprising way of exploiting film with sound. Unfortunately for us, the scene required no speech from Sarah Bernhardt. The sound of clanking swords for the episode was recorded on Edison wax cylinders and played in synchronization with the film from behind the screen. According to several historians it was a successful venture. It is reported that a sound performance of Co-

quelin Aine in *Cyrano* had been featured as part of the exhibition, as well as Rejane in a scene from *Les Précieuses Ridicule*. Following these two were a film of baritone Victor Maurel in arias from Verdi's *Falstaff* and Mozart's *Don Giovanni*.

The legend persists that Bernhardt filmed and recorded theatrical excerpts for Leon Gaumont and Henri Lioret in synchronized sound. Harry M. Geduld, in "The Birth of the Talkies" (Bloomington: Indiana University Press, 1975, p. 58), mentions sound-on-cylinder films of Bernhardt and Gabrielle-Charlotte Rejáne produced by the

Gaumont Company in 1908, using their Chronophone system. Patented as early as 1902, the process synchronized the recordings to a motion picture image, borrowing the compressed-air technology of the Auxetophone for theatrical amplification. By the 1910s, dramatists Edmund Rostand and Henri Lavedam had evidently been hired to write original dramas for a series of Gaumont Phono-Scenes featuring major French actors.

It seems that Sarah was also one of the first actors to integrate film with live theater. Edmond Stoullig's *Les annales du théâtre et de la musique* for 1900 (Paris: Ollendorff) notes that, "In view of the great 1900 tour of America with Mme. Sarah Bernhardt and M. Coquelin, the fifth scene of the drama by M. Rostand (L'Aiglon) is going to be heightened by a new panoramic effect." "The setting of this scene," he continues, "represents the battlefield of Wagram and the Duke of Reichstadt here evokes the heroes fallen in the field of honor, the cadavers of which are strewn upon the ground. In order to add greater realism to this evocation, it has been conceived of raising the glorious dead of the great army by the voice of the son of the victor of Wagram. The dream of Sarah Bernhardt will be realized in a very vivid and tangible way for the public, by the appearance of soldiers and officers, some real, others obtained by the effects of cinematography." It is not clear from Stoullig's account when the scene was actually altered: The quoted description appeared in future tense as a footnote to the fiftieth Parisian performance of *L'Aiglon* on April 30, 1900, but may imply that the expansion of act v, scene v was planned for the

Independent Films

SARAH BERNHARDT as Hamlet, in the duel scene with Laertes. Length 174 feet.

COQUELIN, as Cyrano de Bergerac. Length 140 feet.

COQUELIN. in Precieuses Ridicules. Length 180 feet.

in addition to the above we have over thirty subjects, approximating 150 feet each, of famous French actors and actresses

The negatives from which these films are made are controlled by the Urban-Eclipse Co., and we have the exclusive rights for the United States

Kleine Optical Co.
52 STATE ST.   Opposite Masonic Temple
CHICAGO,   ILL.
Licensee under the Biograph Patents)

Le Duel d'Hamlet (1900) advertisement for the duel scene between Sarah Bernhardt as Hamlet and Laertes. The only sound recorded for Sarah Bernhardt's film was the clanking of the swords. Coquelin was filmed and recorded in short speaking segments from his popular plays, *Cyrano de Bèrgèrac* and *Précieuses Ridicules.*

upcoming American tour. The fascinating possibilities of cinematographic effects can only be guessed, as none are mentioned in the *New York Times* review of the first American tour performance at the Garden Theater on November 26, 1900.

The novelty of Sarah Bernhardt in moving pictures dominated the early films she made, and little was done to explore the creative potential of film. In the eight years that passed between her duel from *Hamlet* to the one reel of highlights from *La Tosca*, great advances in film technique took place. The simplest elements of motion picture story telling and the evolution of the camera as an instrument of expression rather than of mere record all had to be tediously worked out. Some thought it a serious mistake to have any character appear on the screen without entering the scene full length, feet and all. Sarah's early films consistently make this mistake. *Hamlet, La Tosca, Camille,* and *Queen Elizabeth* were all shot straight on as if from the front row of a theater. There were no close-ups to accentuate facial expression.

In 1908, Albert Calmettes, director of the Film d'Art, who had directed Mounet-Sully successfully in *Oedipus Rex* and Re-jáne in *Madame Sans-Gène,* invited Sarah to do a motion picture of her stage success *La Tosca.* She appeared under his direction in the title role, produced by Charles Jourjon, the president of Société Française des Films and Cinématographs Éclair, a French film manufacturing company. Their facility in Paris was considered to be the very latest in movie studio design, innovatively combining glass-covered shooting stages in one plant with an administrative office, a photographic laboratory, dressing rooms, scenery storage and workshops. They opened an American branch in 1911 called the Éclair American Company that soon joined with the new Universal Film Manufacturing Company in releasing productions from the French parent company.

Most early films were a single reel in length, with a running time of 10–12 minutes. The first significant expansion to multiple reels came from the European studios, notably with the *Fall of Troy,* and other like subjects of sweeping, epic scope. A conspicuous effort at a longer length was Sarah's two-reel version of *Camille.* The agents of the French concern that made the picture loudly proclaimed it in advertising, yet it was not a huge success in America.

"I have conquered a new world — that of the photo play," wrote Sarah to W. F. Connor, her American manager, of her playing *Camille* before the cameras. "I never thought, my dear William, that I would ever be [in] a film, but now that I am in two whole reels of pictures, I rely for my immortality upon these records." She was repeatedly asked to appear in moving pictures but refused most of the offers. It took a great deal of persuasion and $30,000 to induce her to play *Camille* before the camera, but when she finally made up her mind she entered into the arrangements with the enthusiasm of a schoolgirl. She visited motion picture shows in all parts of Paris, spent hours in studios and talked with operators and actors. In a short time she was a walking encyclopedia of information about the new art. *Camille* was rehearsed a few times to get it timed right and then, on a set date, Bernhardt and her powerful company went right through the performance before the cameras in long, single takes. The *Moving Picture World,* March 9, 1912, wrote, "Great genius that she is, she suited herself to her medium and the result is a long series of photographs that are staccato in their expressiveness. The story revealed is as plain as print."

Adolph Zukor, an emigrant lad from Hungary, began his life in America with a fur business in Chicago. He progressed into penny arcades of peep show pictures and photographs but was always looking for something new to market. In Paris, Louis Mercanton had made the four-reel picture with Sarah titled *Queen Elizabeth.* The action followed that of Emile Moreau's play, which had been produced some time before at Bernhardt's theater in Paris. The picture chanced to attract the attention in London of Frank Brockliss, an agent for some American producers. He wrote to Joseph Engel in New York, who then told his friend Frank Meyer, manager of the Western Film Exchange, about the film. Zukor and Engel formed the Engadine Corporation and bought the American rights to *Queen Elizabeth* for $18,000. Zukor got a license from the patents company and called his new firm Famous Players Film Company.

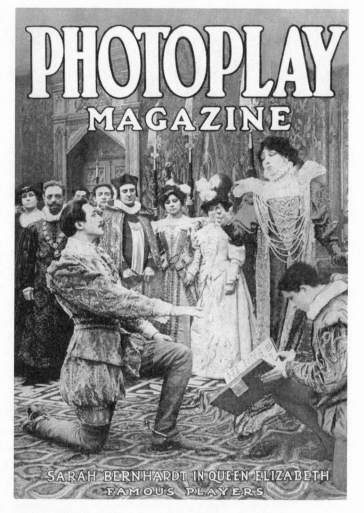

Queen Elizabeth (1912). *Photoplay* magazine issue from September, 1912.

Adolph Zukor, the visionary genius who had the notion that moviegoers would enjoy films that ran for an hour or more, financed the making of *Queen Elizabeth*. His intuition led to the founding of the Famous Players Film Company, which started the fortunes of Paramount Studios.

The Sarah Bernhardt film of *Queen Elizabeth* evolved into a policy of the new company of presenting famous players in famous plays. Supported by Daniel Frohman, one of the greatest names in the theater world, the idea quickly grew. Frohman brought to the growing motion picture business many great plays and the great name performer associated with it, helping to build up the reputation of motion pictures. Sarah Bernhardt's film was their ace card.

"Daniel Frohman Presents" was the headline over the announcement of Sarah Bernhardt in *Queen Elizabeth* when the picture premiered at the Lyceum Theatre in New York City for a promotional showing on July 12, 1912. The picture was quickly sent on road shows around the country, the film being sold on a state's rights basis to buyers who engaged in private retailing of the film to the public. The picture sold for about $80,000, which was a very high profit on Zukor's initial $18,000 investment. The film was a sensation everywhere it was exhibited. Seeing this picture persuaded many other leading stars of the theater to agree to be filmed in their famous plays. The ensuing three years ushered in what was called a "feature craze": long films that took a whole evening to show.

Because of the film's success, Lou-Tellegen, who had been Sarah's leading man for several years, permanently left her employment to pursue a film career in Hollywood.

The front cover of *Motography*, vol. 14, Chicago, July 17, 1915, no. 3.

In *Motography*, a motion picture trade magazine from 1915, Zukor is interviewed:

When questioned regarding the possibility of the Famous Players Company releasing tremendous spectacular productions along the line of those contemplated by a recently formed rival organization, President Zukor declared that only such subjects as merit that kind of production will be undertaken, and that personally, he considers them hard to secure, and much prefers to handle the four and five-reel subjects. In this type, famous stars of the legitimate stage may be featured in stories that can easily be told in that length of film. Mr. Zukor seems of the opinion that the producer is taking long chances on hitting the public's fancy when undertaking the extremely long subjects and has much better chances for success by confining himself to shorter films. The reason for this is that in motion pictures the appeal is made to the eye alone and through the eye to the heart; whereas, on the legitimate

stage, where tremendously big spectacles are prepared, not only the eye but the ear may be reached. The actors have, in addition to pantomime and gestures and beautiful stage settings, wonderful variations in color and, above all, spoken lines, that appeal to the ear when aided by a proper musical accompaniment.

In 1912 Sarah made another film version of highlights from a play, this time her stage success *Adrienne Lecouvreur*. By this time she knew sufficient film technique to create the scenario herself.

A year later, after the amputation of her leg, people feared she would never act again. Immediately after recovering from the devastating surgery she filmed another stage success, *Jeanne Doré*. By this time film technique had advanced enough to creatively obscure her lameness.

Raymond Bernard, son of Tristan Bernard, who wrote the play, had made his

The front cover of *Movie Picture Stories*, January 12, 1917, featured a photograph of Sarah Bernhardt in *Jeanne Doré*.

stage debut opposite Sarah in the role of Jacques Doré and played the same part in the film. He remembered the film was made in two weeks.

During the height of World War I Sarah created her only original film made specifically for motion pictures, *Mères Françaises*, known in America as *Mothers of France*. Many scenes were filmed near the front lines in Paris and in front of the bombed Rheims cathedral.

Sarah often viewed current films in release, and she had a great enthusiasm for the daredevil stuntwoman Pearl White, star of the cliff-hanging serials *The Perils of Pauline*, *The Exploits of Elaine*, *Pearl of the Army* and many others. On January 14, 1917, director Edward Jose of Astra took his *Pearl of the Army* company down to Savannah, Georgia, and the trip resulted in a remarkable tribute from Sarah to Pearl White's fame. She was playing an engagement at the Savannah theater and, hearing that Miss White was in town, sent word that she would like to have White call upon her in her dressing room at the theater after the evening's performance.

Miss White accepted the invitation and, through an interpreter, had an extended interview with Sarah, who told the serial queen that her fame was as widespread in France as it was in the United States. Sarah told her she could not resist the opportunity of making her acquaintance, especially as she had herself seen with pleasure *The Mysteries of New York*, as the serial *The Exploits of Elaine* was titled when released in France. No doubt Sarah, like millions of other women, projected herself into the fabulous, weekly escapades endured by Pearl White as she dove in submarines, dangled from aerial wires and barely survived flights in sabotaged airplanes.

Her final appearance in a dramatic mo-

Mères Françaises (*Mothers of France*) 1917. *Moving Picture World* published this print ad proclaiming the American release of the film to distributors.

tion picture is one of the most incredible stories of indomitable courage ever displayed. In 1923 she became deathly ill, and in her final weeks of life, a film studio was installed on an entire floor of her home on the Boulevard Pereire. For a number of days scenes were filmed for *La Voyante (The Clairvoyant)*. Up to the final hours of her life the cameras turned, filming her in scenes with Mary Marquet, Lili Damita and Harry Baur. Sarah died before her work could be completed, and Jeanne-Marie Laurent stepped in to double for Bernhardt in the few remaining scenes, performing in Sarah's costume with her back to the camera. In this surrogate fashion, *La Voyante* was eventually completed.

Le Duel d'Hamlet (1900)

Act V, Scene II; From the Schwob-Morand translation of Hamlet; Produced and directed by Clement Maurice; Copyrighted in the U.S. in 1908 by the Kleine Optical Company

Cast: Sarah Bernhardt as Hamlet; Pierre Magnier as Laertes

Sarah spent the opening years of the twentieth century touring in *Hamlet*, one of the few women to play the title role. She had commissioned a new French translation of the play by Eugène Morand and Marcel Schwob. They provided her with a prose translation faithful to the original.

Elizabeth Robins in *North American Review,* December 1900, wrote about

the magnetism, the untranslatable fascination that Madame Bernhardt exercises over her public in whatever part she chooses to appear. But, granting the artistic handicap in this particular undertaking — namely, that Hamlet here is a woman and has not Shakespeare to speak — it is interesting to see what special aptitudes the great Frenchwoman brought to her task. Among the most notable of these is her wonderful mastery of sheer poise, that power she has of standing stock still for an indefinite length of time with perfect ease and grace, never shifting from her ground, and equally never ceasing for a moment to be dramatic. It was when she stood so, her feet firmly planted, making only occasional use of sparing, clean-cut gesture, that she came nearest, I should say, to the effect that the artist in her wanted to produce. Here, again and again, one recognized her faculty of keen observation and paid tribute to the accomplished technique that translated her knowledge into action at times so vivid and yet sober. But there will be those, even among Madame Bernhardt's warm admirers, who will feel that, in this version of *Hamlet*, the great tragedy has been drained of its dignity, as well as robbed of its mysterious charm. It is as if, upon some moonlit, spectral scene, the noonday sun burst suddenly, routing the shadow legions, showing alluring alleys to be only sheep paths, and infinite distances to be barred and bounded by the common things of day.

She opened in the play in May 1899 in Paris, and spent the next two years bringing the show to London, Scotland, Switzerland, Austria and Hungary.

Le Duel d'Hamlet (1900), poster for the Phono-Cinema Theatre films featuring France's top theater and opera stars recorded in an early form of sound motion pictures. The performers' voices were recorded on wax cylinders played in synchronization with the projected image.

Sometime during that tour, at the age of 56, she made her film debut. In 1900, she filmed the brief duel from *Hamlet*, more as a technological experiment than a work of art. This staging was the first time any part of *Hamlet* was filmed and was the second film produced based on Shakespeare. Sarah filmed only the single scene, not the entire play.

The motion picture was part of a program devised by Mme. Marguerite Chenu. It is she to whom we are indebted for a record of Sarah, young and graceful. This film was exhibited at the great Paris Exposition Universelle de 1900 which was attended by 50,860,801 visitors who came to see 76,000 exhibitors. Mme. Chenu built for the exposition the first talkie theater and the Phono-Cinema-Theatre. This was Mme. Chanu's enterprising way of exploiting film with sound. Unfortunately, the scene required no speech from Sarah Bernhardt. The sound of clanking swords for the episode was recorded on phonograph wax cylinders and played in synchronization with the film from behind the screen. Ac-

Le Duel d'Hamlet (1900), frame enlargement showing Sarah Bernhardt as Hamlet striking the fatal blow to Laertes.

cording to several historians it was a successful venture.

The film begins with the characters from the play standing motionless in tableau. Sarah is seen in manly attire on a small stage. The duel with Laertes begins and, after fierce swordplay, ends with the stabbing death of Hamlet's adversary. Sarah swoons into the conveniently waiting arms of Hamlet's attendants, then is lifted and carried off screen to the left, exhausted by the ordeal.

The film is preserved in many archives around the world.

La Tosca (1908)

Produced in France by Société Française des Films and Cinématographes Éclair with Film d'Art; U.S. Library of Congress Copyright 10-1-12, 41 prints; Based on the play by Victorien Sardou; Scenario by André Calmettes; Directed by André Calmettes; Length one reel, about 12 minutes, hand colored

Cast: Sarah Bernhardt as Flora Tosca, Edouard de Max, Lucien Guitry, Paul Mounet

The story begins with Angelotti, an escaped political prisoner, hiding in the Roman church of Sant'Andrea della Valle, where the artist Mario Cavaradossi is working on a

THE HOUSE
OF FEATURES

UNIVERSAL FEATURES

225 WEST 42ND. ST.
NEW YORK CITY

A FILM D'ART

Another Feat in Feature Production
NOW READY FOR STATE RIGHTS RELEASE

THE DIVINE

Sarah Bernhardt

IN

—LA TOSCA—

Victorien Sardou's Greatest Drama

When thoughts and speech of film men turn to talk of trade one name reigns
supreme, pre-eminent and unapproached in genius of inspirational acting, SARAH
BERNHARDT.
Yet what avails this Divinity of Art were it not as super-excellently produced?
Announce the fact that it is a Film D'Art and a supreme confidence of the production
rests in their minds. 'Tis a combination Unapproachable.
No drama of all the ages is so adapted to the silent stage. No tragedy contains so
many striking situations wherein not a part of power is lost through lack of speech.

THE ONLY WAY—WIRE!

UNIVERSAL FEATURES 225 West 42nd Street New York City, N. Y.

La Tosca (1908) advertising poster from the original release in the United States.

painting of Mary Magdalene. Angelotti recognizes Mario as an old friend. Mario gives him the keys to his villa, where he can find refuge. Tosca, a famous singer, is Mario's lover. She arrives and becomes enraged with jealousy when she realizes the model for the image of Mary Magdalene is her rival, Marchesa Attavanti. Scarpia, the police chief arrives in pursuit of Angelotti. He is greatly attracted to Tosca and, discovering her jealousy, falsely suggests that Mario is having an affair with the model. This prompts Tosca to rush to Mario's villa, where Angelotti has sought refuge. Scarpia follows in pursuit.

At the apartment of Mario at the Farnese Palace, Scarpia has summoned Tosca for interrogation while Mario undergoes torture in the next room. As Mario cries out in agony, Tosca discloses the hiding place of Angelotti. She pleads for Mario's life. Scarpia agrees to release him if Tosca will

yield to his advances. Realizing this is the only solution, Tosca agrees. Scarpia proposes to write a "safe conduct" note, which will allow the two lovers to leave the country after they go through with a fake execution of Mario. He promises to arrange for the firing squad to use blank bullets. While his back is turned, Tosca stabs him to death.

At dawn Mario is led to his execution. Tosca tells him the execution will be faked and afterward they will escape. She adds that he must put on a convincing imitation of death. The execution squad fires, Mario falls, and the soldiers depart. Tosca rushes to him but finds that Scarpia had deceived her and the bullets used were real ones. Soldiers find the murdered body of Scarpia and advance on Tosca. She jumps to her death from a parapet, vowing to meet Scarpia before God.

Today, *La Tosca* is best known as the opera by Puccini. However, the original play acquired celebrity status long before the creation of the opera version. This was mainly due to the fact that Sarah Bernhardt performed the title role so powerfully. Since 1886, *La Tosca* was one of her greatest stage successes.

The play was written by Victorien Sardou (1831–1908), a French dramatist and author of some 70 plays. The motion picture is based on this version of the story. His light comedies and pretentious historical pieces made him quite popular, but later his reputation declined. His best farce comedy is *Divorces* (1880, tr. 1881). Among his other melodramas based loosely on history were *Patrie* (1869, tr. 1915) and *Fédora* (1882, tr. 1883), in which Sarah Bernhardt made her return to the stage in Paris.

Sardou's other plays written for her are *La Tosca* (1887, tr. 1925), the source of Puccini's opera, and *Cléopâtre* (1890).

Early in 1908 Sarah immortalized her creation of *La Tosca* in motion pictures. Bernhardt was the first to bring *La Tosca* to the cinema screen. André/Albert Calmettes, director of the Film d'Art, who had successfully directed Mounet-Sully in *Oedipus Rex*, and Rejane in *Madame Sans-Gène*, directed the film in one reel which was 10 to 12 minutes in length.

The *Société Film d'Art* produced the motion picture. The company had operated from 1908 through 1912. It was the first highbrow movement in films, aiming to produce film versions of famous plays. The films were very popular, helping to generate a higher class of film audience. The productions were static in the extreme, photographed from a single angle as if from the front row of a theater, with little or no intercutting of shots within a scene.

Other film directors of the same time had already developed the full-screen syntax still used today, but Film d'Art tried to merely photograph stage performances. As film they make no use of the language of the cinema and are purely theatrical. As a record of the French theater of the time they are invaluable documents.

Sarah was so horrified by the film that, upon the death of Victorien Sardou, she attempted to buy up all existing prints and demanded that the negatives should be destroyed. A few years later she learned that others who saw value in the production had thwarted the attempt. The film was widely distributed over several continents.

In *The Moving Picture World*, October 19, 1912, G. F. Blaisdelle wrote,

> Bernhardt has been on the stage for over half a century, and in this film we see her in one of her most successful plays. It may even be classed as one of her favorite plays, the fact that she appears in it is sufficient to indicate that. It is well known that Mme. Bernhardt bears the reputation of doing just those things that suit her own fancy and of looking with impatience on opinions that

Top right: A frame enlargement from a scene from the motion picture *La Tosca* (1908). *Bottom right: La Tosca* (1908). Sarah as Flora Tosca, having just killed the evil Scarpia.

conflict with her own. If aught need be said in extenuation of this attitude her pre-eminence, as an exponent of the dramatic art, will be ample justification.

In transferring this play to the screen, Mme. Bernhardt took pains to secure adequate support. M. De Max has the role of Scarpia, M. Deneubourg is Mario Cavaradossi, and M. Maury is Angelotti. Without question the one scene that stands out above all others is that where Scarpia, the chief of police, approaches La Tosca and puts out his arms to embrace her. La Tosca drives a knife into his breast. The passport is torn from the stiffening fingers; two great candlesticks are placed at the head of the body, and a large crucifix is taken from the wall and laid on the breast of the man who stood between La Tosca and happiness.

The action is fast. That it is interesting is proved by the fact that the two reels seem unusually short. There is no sterner test than this of the holding quality, or to use a much-abused word, the gripping quality of a film. To compress into forty minutes the essentials of this great story necessarily involves the elimination of minor factors. So we have preserved the really vital scenes. If there is an absence of perfect clarity in one or two of the opening scenes, the path of the drama is rapidly smoothed as the plot proceeds.

La Tosca is said to be in the Cinémathèque Française, in Paris.

La Dame aux Camélias (Camille) (1911)

Released in U.S. by the French-American Film Company February 24, 1912; Produced by Le Film d'Art Society in France; From the novel and play of the same name be Alexandre Dumas Fils; Scenario by Henri Pouctal; Directed by André Calmettes or Henri Pouctal; Cinematography by Clément Maurice; Length: 1 reel, about 12 minutes; Hand colored

Cast: Sarah Bernhardt as Marguerite Gautier; Lou-Tellegen as Armand Duval; Paul Capellani as Sadoul; Charmeroy; Suzanne Seylor; Henri Esfontaines; Henri Pouctal; Pitou

On April 11, 1911, *Moving Picture World* issued to all of their subscribers a news flash proclaiming, "Éclair Presents Mme. Bernhardt in Pictures." The article explained, "Time and again it has been suggested that the last word in motion picture enterprise would be to induce Mme. Sarah Bernhardt to pose for the motion picture camera. While it has been noticed that the Divine Sarah appeared before the camera, it has not been generally announced that the Éclair Company was the fortunate company to secure her services. That, however, is the fact about the matter and that fortunate company now announces that it will soon release the picture in which Mme. Bernhardt appears, which will be *Camille*. It is also announced by the same company that Mme. Rejane has been secured for a motion picture revival of Sardou's comedy, *Madam Sans Gene*. In both pictures the stars are supported by a distinguished cast."

Moving Picture World, February 10, 1912, again detailed information about the film, explaining, "Mme. Bernhardt has always regarded her rendition of 'Camille' as her best character portrayal. But it was with great difficulty that she was induced to repeat her performance for motion pictures. She did consent, however, and entered into the task with such enthusiasm that it was only with great difficulty that her efforts were made to conform to the limitations of the camera. The result is a remarkable motion picture, through the agency of which thousands who have never before witnessed her performance on the speaking stage, will be able to see the world's greatest actress in her favorite roles."

This was Sarah's first successful film.

She was paid $30,000, a large sum for the time. In spite of the fact that she was not pleased with her earlier film, *La Tosca*, she decided to film a part of this famous stage play that she had performed for more than thirty years.

The stars went to Neuilly-sur-Seine for the filming in 1911. The filmed version was made in one big take in a single day and printed on two reels.

The film was a turning point in that it attracted an upper class of audiences to early moving picture houses. An amusing legend persists that Sarah fainted when she saw herself in the film.

Jean Cocteau, on viewing *Camille* years later, paid Sarah a somewhat dubious compliment: "I recommend to those who cannot admit the existence of sacred monsters, that they go to New York and see the film of Madame Sarah Bernhardt. What actress will play the great amoureuses better than Sarah in this film? None. And when it is over, we find ourselves back in modern life, like the diver who returns to the surface after having come face to face with a giant devil fish in tropic seas."

The scenario does not tell the complete story. It opens in the cottage outside Paris where Marguerite and Armand have set up housekeeping. The film story begins with the older Duval (Armand's father) arriving at the cottage and begging Marguerite to give Armand up. This she finally consents to do, writing Armand a note renouncing her love for him and leaving. Then the scene changes to a party at Prudence's apartment. Armand comes in and denounces Marguerite, throwing a deck of playing cards into her face. This is followed by Marguerite's death scene in her apartment.

Bernhardt's performance in this brief film, regardless of what she may have been like on the stage, was one of the most elaborate ever to grace the screen. For sheer melodramatic acting, Bernhardt in *Camille* reached the ultimate in this film. All the

La Dame aux Camélias (1911), also known as *Camille*. Sarah Bernhardt as Marguerite Gautier, embracing Lou-Tellegen as Armand Duval, in the early days of their ill-fated romance.

grand gestures — hands flailing, chest beating and eye rolling were used in abundance. Sarah played in a completely unrestrained fashion, a style that was probably well suited to the stage but appeared exaggerated on the screen. There is one notable exception: In the moment of Marguerite's death, while held in Armand Duval's arms, with her hands entwined around his neck, Sarah simply lets her hand go limp, dropping a handkerchief. Her face is completely turned away from the audience, and she telegraphs the moment of death with this simple, elegant gesture. Armand loosens his embrace for a moment, and Sarah nearly falls but is caught

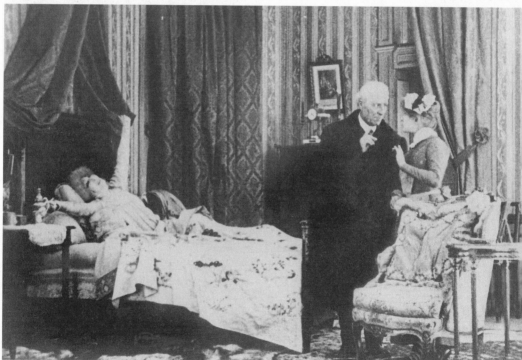

La Dame aux Camelias (1911). *Top:* Sarah Bernhardt as Marguerite Gautier at the moment when Armand Duval's father implores her to renounce her love for his son. *Bottom:* Sarah Bernhardt as Marguerite Gautier, her love for life temporarily rejuvenated by the adoration of Armand Duval.

back in an instant by Armand and gently lowered to the floor.

In a review in *The New York Dramatic Mirror*, 1912, an anonymous reporter stated that

> Madame Bernhardt proves in this production, as had been anticipated, her wonderful adaptability to the peculiar forms of expression required for finished picture acting. It is the mark of the great artist, demonstrated more vividly, if anything, than is possible on the theatre stage. With the art of which she is so much the master, she appears in the picture to be the living embodiment of *Camille*, unconscious of camera or of supposed spectators and conveying, not by pantomime, but by natural and significant actions and expression the progress of the story. The culmination comes in the death scene, which Bernhardt's art renders in a way distressing, but tremendously impressive and convincing. She is standing in Armand's embrace with her face hidden from view by her hand drooping and falling like the flower from which Marguerite's sobriquet was derived. Fortunately the picture adaptation of *Camille* has been modeled with considerable success after the technique of the photoplay as developed by the experience and genius of those who have led in the growth in this new art. Had the adaptation been merely or even largely a reproduction of the action of the stage play minus the words it must have proved disappointing even with Mme. Bernhardt's great ability and prestige. But this pitfall has been avoided. The story is told by the photoplay method and told quite clearly, although it could have been more forceful perhaps and certainly more explicit in some of the scenes, as, for instance, the fragment of the duel scene, which, however, may have been cut down to a mere indefinite indication of the end of the duel, to avoid fancied interference of troublesome censors. In this, however, the producers were probably too cautious at the expense of the picture's art — a thing that was hardly necessary in a production of such distinction. In one other respect, also, the picture fails to realize the most advanced development of the photoplay. This is in the too numerous and too

La Dame aux Camélias (1911). Sarah Bernhardt as Marguerite Gautier, her face washed with tears, as she writes a farewell letter to Armand Duval, the great love of her life.

> explanatory interscriptions (subtitles), many things being announced in words that are clearly understandable from the actions themselves. At times these advance explanations of what is to follow are annoying to the spectator and rob the picture story of its interest. All this, however, is no fault of Mme. Bernhardt, and will not prevent the motion picture record of her interpretation of *Camille* from being one of the masterpieces of the photoplay, destined to be preserved for posterity. The settings are magnificent and realistic and the support excellent. The photography also is of the best French quality.

An article in *Moving Picture News* of March 1912, contains the following review under the caption *Sarah the Divine in Moving Pictures*: "*Camille* was never more pitifully eloquent than in this dumb record.

La Dame aux Camélias (1911). Sarah Bernhardt as Marguerite Gautier, declaring the depths of her love to Armand Duval, played by Lou-Tellegen, in the fateful moments before passing away.

Sarah Bernhardt played with wonderful fire and expressiveness. Great genius that she is, she suited herself to her medium and the result is a long series of photographs that are staccato in their expressiveness. The story is revealed as plain as print. *Camille* is a perfect photoplay. The story lends itself to the purposes of the camera, and Bernhardt is eloquent in every movement. Someone has said that the pictures fairly crackle with life and projects wireless messages to the spectators. All over Europe the photoplay *Camille* is a sensation and Americans

La Dame aux Camélias. Sarah Bernhardt as Marguerite Gautier, in the final throes of death within the arms of her lover, Armand Duval, played by Lou-Tellegen.

are eagerly awaiting the release of these reels, which are now in the control of the French-American Film Company which is rapidly disposing of State rights."

Sarah could hardly wait to see an exhibition screening of the film after it was prepared. When the operator started and the photoplay began to transpire upon the screen she was almost hysterical with excitement. After seeing the two reels she insisted that they be run a second time, and this was done. At the finish she turned to Edmond Rostand, who accompanied her, and asked, "What next for me?"

The Film d'Art Company began production of films in 1903. Literary figures and the leading actors of the Comédie Française fathered this motion picture, the first of highbrow movements. Film d'Art simply transferred a play to the screen, filming exact duplications of the stage performances, with little of the creative freedom the cinema was utilizing at the hands of many other producers at the time. The movement ultimately failed financially as well as artistically.

As films, most of these stage-celebrity pictures make no use of the language of cinema and are redeemed for us chiefly by our own amazement and excitement at seeing a legendary figure and watching a dead theater period come to life before our eyes. As records, they are more precious for theater historians and actors than any other documentation available, of those actors who had allowed a movie camera to be set up in front of them. Something tangible and useful remains of these actors from the theater who made films.

According to *The Moving Picture World*, February 10, 1912, "These pictures are remarkable in more than one respect. They are the product of the famous *Society Film D'Art of Paris* and were enacted before the camera by nearly all the actors and actresses who appeared in the first productions of these respective plays on a French-speaking stage."

In an article called "Music for the Picture," by Clarence E. Sinn, in *The Moving Picture World* (vol. 13, no. 9, August 31, 1912, p. 871), "*Camille* was never shown in silence. At the very least there was a piano; at the most, an orchestra. The score for Camille, as given here, is loaded with old chestnuts, but it is handy for telegraphing the mood of a scene at its very opening, a practice that is still followed by the makers of film today. I have been managing the house and leading the orchestra since June 3rd. Am enclosing my program for the Sarah Bernhardt film *Camille*. The manager of these pictures was good enough to ask for a list, saying it fit the picture better than any yet found. Hope it may be of use."

Camille First Act

1. Waltz lento until Camille ad Armand alone, then:
2. "The Flatterer" (Chaminade) twice through.
3. "Scarf Dance."
4. "Serenade" (Puerner) or "Spring Song" (Mendelssohn).

Camille Second Act

5. "Confidence" (Mendelssohn). Twice.
6. "Berceuse" (Godard) or Waltz lento until title: "Camille's home in the country."
7. "Evening Star" (Tannhäuser), until Armand's father leaves Camille.
8. "Calm as the Night" (Bohm), until next title.
9. "Song without Words" (Tchaikovsky). to end of act. Tempo according to the action.
10. "La Bohème Fantaisie" (Puccini) until Camille is out of bed.
11. "Barcarolle" (Tales of Hoffman), until Camille's arm drops to her side.
12. "Ase's Death" (Peer Gynt Suite — Grieg), until end.

Early nickelodeon movie theaters provided musical accompaniment with pianists near the screen. The producers of _Camille_ provided a suggested score of old musical chestnuts that fit the mood of each scene.

W. Stephen Bush wrote in _The Moving Picture World_, March 2, 1912,

It may well be doubted whether money would have induced Sarah Bernhardt, the greatest of living actresses, to play _Camille_ before a moving picture camera. To such a passionate lover of her art, it must have seemed glorious to defy the limitations of space and time and have the whole world as her audience. The cinematograph is indeed a monument more enduring than brass and it is far more ornamental and useful as well. The immortality conferred by the motion picture is well worth having.

It is not the smallest tribute to the genius of Sarah Bernhardt to say that her art loses nothing in its transmission to the little strips of celluloid. The gifts of other noted artists do not shine as well in the motion pictures as they do on the speaking stage, just as some talented singers please us in opera, but are heard to poor advantage in the gramophone. The splendor of Sarah Bernhardt's art remains undimmed in the photoplay.

To paint the lily, or throw perfume on the violets is no more of a wasteful and ridiculous excess than to pile up new ad-

jectives in praise of the genius of Sarah Bernhardt. It is true of her, indeed, that age cannot wither, nor custom stale her infinite variety. To body forth Dumas' conception of _Camille_, an exuberance of youth is needed. _Camille_ first wins our sympathy and stirs our profoundest pity because her youth is cast in endless shade, though, of course, her noble sacrifice deepens the feeling. She possesses all the gayety of her kind: the animal joy of living, but not untouched by a certain womanly grace and sweetness. Until she meets Armand, her finer nature has lain dormant, she was a beauteous butterfly and the sins she committed were of the kind which Christian charity is most ready to forgive. Sarah Bernhardt, by a splendid display of her genius, makes us understand the profound change that came over _Camille_ after Armand entered her life. With consummate art she shows the ennobling and sobering influence of a sincere love. We see how the careless and frivolous demimondaine of the better sort becomes a true woman, whose soul grows stronger as her body turns chaste. One who patiently bears suffering and humiliation and sacrifices her happiness for the sake of others.

It is, however, in the portrayal of the tragic element that the divine Sarah rises to the most dazzling heights of the mimic art. How subtle is the touch by which she gives us the first hint of the fatal nature of her malady, when the first reel has scarcely begun. This marvelous power in developing the tragic element is finely sustained throughout until it culminates in a veritable triumph of acting in the last scene.

To see these two reels is to realize to the fullest extent the art and power of Sarah Bernhardt and no greater boon could be offered to the theater-goer of today. Every audience looking at these films will be stirred as deeply as those who saw Sarah Bernhardt act in the flesh. It goes without saying that these pictures will gain new friends for the motion picture by the thousands and that directly or indirectly every branch of the motion picture industry will have its benefit from them. I only hope operators everywhere will be kind to the pictures and not try to run them at a Saturday night rate of speed. There is no room anywhere for effects, but music of the right kind will be most acceptable. Pathos should be its dominant note.

The film is in the Museum of Modern Art, New York.

Sarah Bernhardt à Belle Isle (Sarah Bernhardt at Home) (1912)

Documentary; 2 reels; Manufacturer: Film d'Art

According to Henri Langlois, director of the Cinémathèque Française in Paris, December 4, 1959, Sarah Bernhardt made a film at her home in Belle Isle, in which she and Sir Basil Zaharof were photographed.

According to William M. Embolden in *Sarah Bernhardt, Artist and Icon*, "the whole world was interested in this rare creature whose life and exploits were known to them through film, tours, biographies, and her own autobiography. If press coverage was so well received, it seemed logical to make a film of Sarah on her Brittany Island. Who could resist being invited into the home of a women who was the world's foremost actress, a painter and sculptress of considerable talent, a keeper of wild beasts."

The film consists of intimate glimpses of Sarah among the rocky heights with a group of devoted friends as they climb the rocky shore cliffs. Included are Sir Basil Zaharof and his son Maurice. Then Sarah is shown rising at the dawn of day, tending to lobster pots, and feeding chickens, ducks, geese and pigs like a farm hand. Scenes of lunch with her family present Sarah at her gracious best. She fishes, plays tennis, and converses with local fishermen whom she befriended during periods of famine on the island.

In *The Moving Picture World*, July 31, 1915, an anonymous reviewer wrote, "Finally, the great actress is pictured in her den overlooking the sea. There she entertains lavishly and showers adorations and adulations upon her pets. Altogether the pictures show Bernhardt as she really is in the flesh, her charities are brought out in bold relief.

"The Photoplay Releasing Company is disposing of state and territorial rights very fast, it is said. It is planned to release the picture just prior to the Bernhardt opening at the New Amsterdam Theater in New York City, on September 18. From this playhouse in the Metropolis, the actress will make a triumphant tour to the Pacific Coast. It will be her final tour. The filmed Bernhardt, at motion picture prices, will follow the Bernhardt in the flesh (at $5.00 per seat) wherever she appears on her American and Canadian tours."

The film was initially hand-tinted in colors that enhance the mood of each scene, a film printing technique that was commonplace at the time.

In *Motography* 1915, a reviewer by the name of Neil G. Caward wrote,

When Aaron M. Gollos, president of the Photoplay Releasing Company, purchased the negative of the two-reel feature film, *Sarah Bernhardt at Home,* thereby securing the sole right to exhibit the picture in the

STATE RIGHTS BUYERS

The Photoplay Releasing Company

414 Mallers Building, Chicago

announce that

by an arrangement made with Mme. Bernhardt and the Belgian Red Cross Society through William F. Connor, manager of Mme. Bernhardt, this Company has secured the North American rights to the two reel picture, entitled

Sarah Bernhardt at Home

Never before has the **Divine Sarah** posed for the camera on the subject treated here. The film shows with marvelous minuteness the simple home-life of the greatest living actress of the age.

Madame Bernhardt is shown in an ex-cellently staged production among the grandeurs of her home life on Picturesque Belle Isle, Brittany.

Madame Bernhardt will make a final tour of America this fall. She opens in New York, Sept. 18th and will play every large city in America at tremendous prices.

You can release this picture while she is playing in your territory and make big money.

Write, wire or telephone for territory and prices

THE PHOTOPLAY RELEASING CO.
♥ ♥ A·M·GOLLOSPRES· ♥ ♥

Newspaper advertisements spread over two-page positions proclaimed the appearance of the film *Sarah Bernhardt at Home*. The film was booked into towns prior to her tours to create public excitement.

United States, he did every admirer of the divine Sarah a tremendous favor, for the picture gives the innumerable Bernhardt admirers a more intimate glimpse of their idol than has ever been offered them in any other way."

Photographically the feature is a gem, every scene being clear as a crystal and wonderful as to detail, while the splendid photography is further aided by the delicate tinting and superb scenery.

Every intimate detail of the great actress' home life is minutely pictured. One sees her arrival with her son, Maurice, at their beautiful home in Brittany and the welcome which is given her by the tenants and peasants of her estate.

After disposing of her baggage, Madame Bernhardt, remembering that a sea voyage is often tiresome, orders that tea be served to her guests and then the company sets out for a trip over the vast estate, the owner being greeted with cheers and handclasps by every peasant and tenant with whom she comes in contact. The reason for this is that the simple residents of Brittany fairly wor-

ship the ground their famous mistress walks upon.

Beautiful glimpses are given of the old fort which Madame Bernhardt has had transformed into a palatial home. One views with interest the deep-pool and dragnet prawning, for the divine Sarah fairly revels in herself catching those denizens of the deep that inhabit the waters bordering her estate. The fantastic and unusual caves, grottos and rocks that abound in the vicinity of the Bernhardt domicile are all pictured, and after the famous tragedienne has acted as hostess at a shooting party, she is seen rambling over the rocky ledges in the vicinity of her home, finally cut off by the rising tide and forced to clamber hastily back to higher ground. Returning home she enjoys a game of tennis, her sprightliness being truly amazing when one remembers that she is no longer young.

The second reel of the feature includes scenes that show Bernhardt's ability as a sculptress, when she is seen modeling a bust of Rostand, the famous author of "*Cyrano de Bèrgèrac*," the play she made famous by featuring it in her repertoire. Her library of over six thousand volumes is a favorite nook in which the celebrated tragedienne finds much comfort and her flower garden gives pleasure, not alone to her, but to all her friends.

When the sardine fishing, by which many of the tenants on the Bernhardt estate make their living, was for a time impossible, Bernhardt, at no little expense to herself, established a co-operative bakery at which all her tenants were provided bread and other food at less than half price. We see the tenants gathering to do her homage, as a token of appreciation for her kindness to the poverty stricken fisher-folk. The gala occasion closes with a folk-dance in which all the natives take part and at the end, Madame Bernhardt bestows flowers, autographs and other little tokens upon her friends, each of which is treasured and held as a sacred relic by the person receiving it.

The film ends with an intimate and close-up glimpse of the great actress in her cozy corner, enjoying a play spell with "Bellidor," her pet Pomeranian.

Taken as a whole, the film is of tremendous interest, picturing as it does, that portion of Madame Bernhardt's life which the public has never glimpsed or seldom even considered. Undoubtedly the film will be tremendously popular wherever shown, for this year, when Bernhardt again visits this

This frame enlargement from the film *Sarah Bernhardt at Home* showed her relaxing with her pet Pomeranian.

country in person, newspapers will be devoting whole pages to her remarkable career and talent. The state rights buyer who can offer exhibitors in his territory, a feature of such wide appeal, ought to be able to make a fortune, due to the unusual timeliness of the subject, and to the wonderful talent of the central figure.

Mr. Gollos was able to secure the Bernhardt films through an arrangement with the Belgian Red Cross Society, who are joint owners of the copyright on the picture, Mr. Gollos perfecting his arrangement through William F. Connor, personal manager of Madame Bernhardt.

The film is said to be preserved in the Cinémathèque Française in Paris.

Les Amours de la Reine Elisabeth (Queen Elizabeth) (1912)

Scenario by Emile Moreau based on the play by Emile Moreau; Directed by Louis Mercanton and Henri Desfontaines; 4 reels (50 minutes) Film d'Art; Released in the U.S. July 1912 by Famous Players Film Company

Cast: Sarah Bernhardt as Queen Elizabeth; Lou-Tellegen as James Devereaux, the Earl of Essex; Mlle. Romane as Countess of Nottingham; M. Decoeur as Sir Francis Drake; M. Maxudian as Earl of Nottingham; M. Chameroy as Lord Bacon; Marie-Louise Dorval

After the success of *Camille* there were constant rumors about her signing with other companies to make more motion pictures. These rumors met with a prompt denial from Sarah in a letter to the French-

American Film Company of New York, which was distributing *Camille*. The letter reads as follows:

Gentlemen, I have not posed nor contracted to pose for any motion pictures whatever

GRASP YOUR OPPORTUNITY

WE HAVE A PATENT RIGHT TO PROCLAIM

SARAH BERNHARDT

— *IN THE FILM MASTERPIECE.* —

QUEEN ELIZABETH

IN 4 PARTS

**THE ONLY FEATURE FILM THAT HAS ALL THE
QUALITIES THAT MAKE IT WORTHY OF THE NAME**

FEATURE FILM

**A FEW OF ITS
QUALIFICATIONS**

Prestige

Drawing Power

The Greatest
Actress at her
best.

PerfectProduction

**Five States Sold
Last Week**

———

**MARCUS LOEW
Bought New York**

**FOLLOW HIM AND
YOU CANNOT LOSE**

**WE HAVE BOOKINGS
TO TURN OVER WITH
EACH PURCHASE**

Licensed by Motion Picture Patents Co.

Don't Hesitate — Wire Now and Reap the Reward of Success

Everything Pertaining to This Production Spells Success

FAMOUS PLAYERS FILM CO.

TIMES BUILDING, NEW YORK CITY

F. ZUKOR, Pres.   DANIEL FROHMAN, Man. Director

Trade publications, such as *Moving Picture World,* featured full-page advertisements proclaiming
Queen Elizabeth (1912) a masterpiece with prestige, drawing power and the greatest actress at her
best.

except with the Film d'Art Company of Paris, for whom I have already done *Camille* as a photoplay, the North American rights of which are exclusively controlled by the French-American Film Company of New York. My contract with the Film d'Art Company covers my every appearance for motion pictures.

The story is a fanciful retelling of the tale of the tragic romance between the Queen of England and the Earl of Essex. It begins with a promise of an ardent and not ignoble love. The great Tudor queen, whose heart leaps with patriotic joy when in her prime she hears of the defeat of the Spanish Armada. She is triumphantly borne out by her attendants on a raised litter. After attending a performance of Shakespeare with Essex, a fortune-teller is conducted into the palace to predict an unhappy future for the queen. She tells Essex that he will die on the scaffold. The queen, greatly upset by the forecast, places her ring on Essex's finger, with instructions to return it if he needs her help. She promises to save him however great his fault may be.

However, Essex is in love with the Countess of Nottingham. Her husband discovers them in a lover's embrace, and swears vengeance. He instigates a charge of treason upon Essex in the form of an anonymous letter to the queen. She accidentally discovers Essex has been unfaithful to her with the countess and orders his arrest. Sickened by this turn of events, she begs the countess to persuade him to return the ring so that she can save him. The countess does so, and Essex gives her the ring. Nottingham prevents his wife from returning the ring and throws it in the Thames River. Elizabeth

Queen Elizabeth (1912). The opening scene showing the queen, played by Sarah Bernhardt, receiving news of Lord Essex's triumph in battle.

signs his death warrant, believing him to be too proud to ask for clemency.

The sentence is carried out with Essex trembling beneath the sharp edge of the executioner's axe. Grieving with a tortured, royal heart, Elizabeth visits the body in the morgue, where she discovers the ring is missing.

The countess confesses the truth about the interception of the ring. Elizabeth cries, "May God forgive you. I never will!" Learning the truth too late, the queen never has another happy moment. She becomes a vain, old woman, at once wishing flattery and despising it, forbidding the presence of mirrors at the court for fear of learning from the truthful leaded glass the sad revelation of her faded charms and her approaching end. She dies of a broken heart, falling forward from her throne onto a mass of giant pillows.

The final words on the screen "Sic transit gloria mundi" mean "Thus passes away the glory of the world."

In presenting the play on the screen, Bernhardt herself arranged the scenes. She had to reckon with the fact that, whereas a play tells its story primarily by dialogue, a motion picture relies primarily on pictures. The solution to this problem was to present as much of the film action as possible in pantomime and augment it with explanatory titles. The playing of the film was arranged in twenty-three scenes with subtitles.

The year 1912 was the time of the *Titanic* disaster, the discovery of the South Pole, the election of Woodrow Wilson, the

Queen Elizabeth (1912). Lou-Tellegen as Lord Essex recounts the victory of battle to the jubilant queen.

Queen Elizabeth (1912). Sarah Bernhardt and cast in the film that started the feature-length movie standard that revolutionized the budding motion picture industry.

Rosenthal murder in New York, and the eruption of tango and ragtime music.

Queen Elizabeth was filmed in Paris in May of 1912 and premiered at the Lyceum Theatre in New York for a promotional showing to the press and a distinguished audience on July 12, 1912. It was made by Sarah Bernhardt at the age of 77 in an attempt to recoup the staggering financial losses incurred during the twelve-performance theatrical run of the play. It was the biggest film sensation of her cinematic career.

It was filmed during a three-month period utilizing the cast from the stage production. It was a huge hit in Europe and highly influential in America. It is the one film, of the many she made, that has had the widest distribution, the longest availability, and the greatest impact. The film was a pivotal point in motion picture history and had far-reaching consequences. It served to establish the effectiveness of multireel features in an era characterized almost exclusively by one- and two-reel shorts. It raised the moving picture from a low reputation as a sideshow gimmick to a plane on which was won the admiration and loyalty of millions of new followers.

Ambitious nickelodeon manager and fledgling producer Adolph Zukor, Daniel Frohman, Joseph Engel and Edwin Porter formed the Engadine Corporation. They bought the American rights for their Famous Players Company for $18,000, according to *A Million and One Nights* (or

$35,000 according to Adolph Zukor's autobiography), paying the delighted Sarah 10 percent of the gross and $350 a day for personal appearances. Zukor cleared over $80,000 on the film by marketing it as a road show on a state's rights basis, from which he built his later production empire, Paramount Films.

Up to this time most actors considered the movies to be beneath them. The success of *Queen Elizabeth* strengthened the respectability of motion pictures by convincing other theater stars to appear in feature-length adaptations of their successful plays. They saw that it would be to their advantage, that it would arouse popular interest, not only in their productions, but in their personalities as well. What appealed to them most of all was the chance of immortality on celluloid. Their acceptance of cinema, even as a means to record their stage performances for posterity, was an important step in the development of the motion picture industry.

Sarah Bernhardt's happy influence on the American motion picture industry is well expressed in the message sent to her by Adolph Zukor on the tenth anniversary of the founding of Famous Players and signed by twenty-two movie personalities, who included Wallace Reid, Mary Pickford, Gloria Swanson, Anita Stewart, Douglas Fairbanks, William S. Hart, Norma Talmadge, Mary Miles Minter, Pauline Frederick, and Thomas Meighan: "We invite you to visit America as a guest of honor at a great national fete celebrating our industry. This invitation is addressed to you because you were the first great artist to lend her genius to our art. Your example, ten years ago, gave to the motion picture industry the impulse which has raised it to the place of the most important spectacle in the world. Your appearance in *Queen Elizabeth* was a priceless boon to the cinema, just as your appearance on the stage has always been an inspiration for the theatre."

Within *Queen Elizabeth* one can find five distinct variations of the tragic and dramatic styles of acting prevalent at the beginning of the twentieth century. Maxudian, as the Earl of Nottingham, is the clearest survival of an earlier, more calculated, classic style, with hands and eyes several degrees too eloquent, and employing a splendid heaving pattern for his body movements, supporting himself with glances toward the camera audience. Without Maxudian's spirit, the acting of Lord Bacon gives us a classic shell, with a formula of backward looks and steps. Maxudian later played in many important French silents, and he gave a superb performance as Barras in Abel Gance's *Napoléon*.

Bernhardt herself takes this older form, puts real passion and tragedy into it and, even without her rumbling alto, preserves her greatness before us, notably during the agonizing scene when Essex is led to the block. Her gestures, although necessarily broad, are purposeful and complete. They are exaggerated, but they are never awkward.

Lou-Tellegen, as Lord Essex, uses a formless variety of romanticism, feeling nothing and conveying nothing. Mlle. Romain, as the Countess of Nottingham, works with a classic style mixed in slovenly fashion with lapses into naturalism.

In *The Moving Picture World*, August 3, 1912 (pages 428–429), W. Stephen Bush writes, "Historical accuracy, swift and clear action, a sustained splendor of settings and the supreme art of Sarah Bernhardt combine to make this play stand out as a rare and most creditable achievement. It deals with the life of the famous queen in an impressive, masterful manner. The whole performance is marked by dignity and an unmistakable care in the preparation of every detail. The most remarkable part of this play is its accuracy in historical detail. The procession to and from the court was a masterpiece of historical cinematography, in spite

Queen Elizabeth (1912). Elizabeth's advisors accuse Lord Essex of treason.

of the fact that the scenery was painted, when it might just as well have been natural. The mournful pageant itself was true to recorded history even to the headsman's axe being carried with the edge turned away from the Earl, while after his sentence, it is turned toward him."

Of Sarah's performance: "So superb is the art of Sarah Bernhardt that she made her conception, which is that of a passionate women dominated wholly by her affections, seem not impossible." "She exhibited her best powers and won from her audience such keen sympathy and compassion as the real Elizabeth could never have expected.

Sarah Bernhardt rose to the situation in the final scene with consummate art and gave an example of her acting, which will linger in the beholder's memory for many a day.

Queen Elizabeth will win hosts of friends for the motion picture. Two scenes in this feature are especially pathetic and impressive; the last scene in the first reel which shows the leave-taking of the Earl of Essex and the Countess of Nottingham, and the last scene of the third act, portraying the death of the queen."

In *The Theatre Magazine* of 1912, an anonymous reviewer wrote, "Sarah did not merely pose mechanically for a mechanical contrivance, but proceeded to give one of the finest performances of which this greatest living artist is capable."

In *The Moving Picture World*, September 21, 1912, headlines announced, "Sarah Bernhardt Pleased with Pictures." The article went on to report that Sarah said, "It is with a feeling of gratitude that I turn to the

Queen Elizabeth (1912). *Top left:* Sarah Bernhardt in the title role watching the death march to the executioner's block where Essex is to die at the blade of an axe. *Top right:* Sarah Bernhardt in the title role, venturing into the dark tomb to weep over the decapitated remains of Lord Essex, played by Lou-Tellegen. *Below:* The death of the queen.

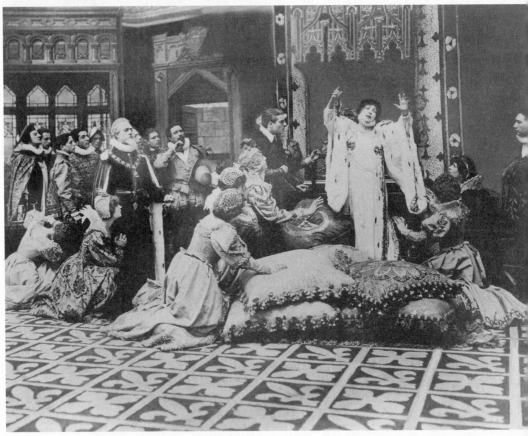

God of genius, to offer him prayer for that wonderful miracle he hath brought about, whereby he hath given men the power to hand down to posterity the greatest success of my career — *Queen Elizabeth*. It is a great joy for me to know that my masterpiece is within the reach of all the people throughout the universe, and I hope it will be appreciated before and long after I am gone."

The film is in the Museum of Modern Art, New York, and a 16mm print and negative are in the Library of Congress.

Adrienne Lecouvreur
(An Actress's Romance) (1913)

Produced by Film d'Art; Library of Congress Copyright 2-3-13 by William F. Connor; Directed by Louis Mercanton and Henri Desfontaines; Scenario by Sarah Bernhardt; Based on an earlier play by Eugene Scribe and Ernest Legouve; Length: 1783 ft, 2 reels, about 24 minutes

Cast: Sarah Bernhardt as Adrienne Lecouvreur; Lou-Tellegen; Henri Desfontaines

The story is biographical, based on the life of actress Adrienne Lecouvreur (1692–1730), covering her tragic love and mysterious death in the time of Louis XV. She was a successful French actress, who, with the help of Michel Baron, changed the traditional acting techniques of the French stage to a natural style.

Her popularity began with her debut at the Comédie Française in 1717. Tragedy ended her love for Maurice de Saxe (1696–1750, marshal of France, and one of the greatest generals of his age. Adrienne's mysterious death was said to be the result of poisoning by her rival, the duchesse de Bouillon. The church refused to give her a Christian burial.

The legend of her life made good subject matter for both the opera *Adriana Lecouvreur* by Francesco Cilea as well as the play by Eugene Scribe and Ernest Legouve.

Augustin Eugène Scribe (1791–1861) was a French dramatist and librettist who was one of the first playwrights to mirror bourgeois morality and life, infusing nineteenth-century French opera and drama with liberal political and religious ideas.

In *The Moving Picture World*, Feb. 1, 1913, an anonymous reviewer wrote, "This is a distinctly French production, based on incidents which are supposed to have occurred in the life of Mme. Adrienne Lecouvreur, a noted and talented actress, very prominent on the French stage during the early part of the eighteenth century. It is said that Madame Sarah Bernhardt has adapted the story for moving picture representations. She herself plays the title part. The distinguished artist, according to reports, regards her role in this story as one of her favorites. The story, as told in the film, is quite complicated, though at the same time, full of life and action. Intrigues, plots, counterplots, treasons and stratagems follow one another in rapid succession. Of course, the name of Bernhardt makes the production attractive to the public, many of whom no doubt saw her in this role on one of her tours through the country."

Because this film seems to be lost, information and photos are scarce. Sarah Bernhardt had appeared in two plays titled *Adrienne Lecouvreur*; the traditional play by Eugène Scribe and Ernest Legouve, and the one which Sarah herself wrote and produced in 1907. Sarah also wrote the adaptation of the story for this motion picture. According to René Jeanne and Charles Ford, the film

Adrienne Lecouvreur (1913) advertising poster details the eleven scenes comprising this motion picture. No known copy is available today.

is an adaptation of the Bernhardt play, the actress anticipating that her film would compete with the Scribe-Legouve film, which starred Julia Bartet in the title role. It was a hit, though a qualified one. Some critics complained of the overlong titles, necessary to clear up confusing plot points. But most reviews called the film and its star "unfailingly impressive" and noted that "the play of her wonderfully expressive features is allowed full scope." Apparently the director permitted more close-ups in this film. One newspaper even praised the "two well-trained dogs" used in the production. Sarah herself complained only of hitting her marks during the filming; she was used to having

an entire stage to work in, and confining herself to the camera's narrow range frustrated her.

Lou-Tellegen made his debut in motion pictures in this film with Sarah. He spent his formative years as a leading man to Sarah Bernhardt in plays and appeared in this, the first of three of her films. Lou was tall, striking in appearance, and photographed superbly. He was greatly admired by American audiences.

Strand Magazine, December 1915, quotes Sarah as saying, "When I first acted before the camera in *Adrienne Lecouvreur* I was afraid the film would be far from successful, the confined area in which I had to

Left: Sarah Bernhardt in the film version of *Adrienne Lecouvreur. Right:* Sarah Bernhardt in the 1880 stage play of *Adrienne Lecouvreur.*

act in order to keep within the focus of the camera, the absence of audience and words, seemed so unreal that I could arouse no enthusiasm. However, I proved to be a bad judge of effects, and was agreeably surprised at the result."

The film appears to be lost; no known prints have been located as of 2003.

Ceux de Chez Nous
(Those at Our House) (1915)

Written and Directed by Sacha Guitry; Length 35–44 minutes

Cast: Sarah Bernhardt; Auguste Rodin; Claude Monet; Camille Saint-Saëns; Edgar Degas; Pierre-Auguste Rodin

Those at Our House was first shown on November 23, 1915, at the Theatre of the Varieties. It is a documentary photographed during the years of 1913 to 1914. Shortly after the start of World War I, Sacha Guitry, already known as a dramatic author, decided to respond to the turbid remarks of German intellectuals, by using an amateur camera to engrave in images for future generations the great personalities who contributed to the prestige of France. The film was shown with commentary by Guitry and his wife, Charlotte Lyses. In 1939 he added a soundtrack with this same commentary. A final version, in collaboration with Frederic Rossif, was created in 1952 as a television special. New images and accompanying notes were added.

Sacha Guitry reflected on the film in the prologue of the soundtrack of the 1939 version

Mesdames and Messieurs, I have the unusual honor of inviting you to the original experience of a hearing of a film that is silent. It is true that I am such a chatterer, like a deaf person who speaks to blind men with this presentation of a silent film. I do not have to even ask you for your indulgence, because it is with your graces that I speak. The film will take you down half the

Ceux de Chez Nous (*Those at Our House*) 1915. Sarah Bernhardt, full of the joy of life, with her son, Maurice, in the film produced by Sacha Guitry.

path, and my spoken description will endeavor to take you down the other half. And God wants that the two paths should meet. The idea had come to me one day that the motion picture could be used to give to the public invaluable information on subjects of interest and allow them to get to know them better.

In 1914 the motion picture was a new, extraordinary invention, an inexhaustible source of surprise and delight. Everyone agreed that it was useful in the service of science. Some twenty-five years ago I was able to document a series of short portraits of those men and women who were outstanding in the field of the arts.

Up to this time the cinema had only shown small comedies, landscapes, animals in motion, and brief clips of famous figures coming and going, much to the amusement of the public. Today we cruelly make fun of these early films, laughing at their ridiculous presentations of certain famous actors, as the cinema too [took] its first steps of prog-

ress. This is like laughing at a child who takes his first steps. Oh, if only this invention had come earlier! What emotion we would have if we could see Michelangelo carving his Moose, or Leonard de Vinci painting the Mona Lisa, the preaching of Basset, Jean of the Fountain writing a fable, Racine, Voltaire, Jean-Jacques Rousseau. If we could only see these faces, the glances of these men, their personal gestures, it would be so beautiful! So, in 1914 I decided to gather those artists from all branches of Art that were the living incarnation of French talent. I called this film "*Those at Our House.*" Twenty-five years ago I showed this film to some few people, and then it lay unseen for another twenty-five years. It is with great emotion I see it again now, reviving for our eyes twelve admirable Frenchmen who were my friends, all but one of whom are deceased.

Noel Simsolo, in an excerpt from the *Book of the Cinema*, 1988, wrote, "The first version of this film comprised sequences taken from a moving car of each celebrity. These images do not exist anymore in the current version. The Guitrys provided a sound accompaniment, in synchronization with the movement of the lips in the images on the film with such exactitude, that the illusion of a 'talking film' had been realized, exceeding the hopes of its makers. The focus is on the presentation of each artist in the act of presenting his or her talent at work. The exception being Sarah Bernhardt, who is presented in various static poses. Her presence in the film was sufficient to the makers. These artists accepted the idea of being recorded by the whim of their friend armed with a camera. Thus enabled, we see Rodin carving, Edmond Rostand writing, the lawyer Henry Robert, improvising a courtroom plea in his kitchen, Antoine directing a scene of *The School of the Women*, Claude Monet doing calculations at a table, Inutile France in his library, Camille Saint-Saëns directing an orchestra and playing the piano, August Renoir painting with sick fingers and sharp eyes while his son Jean mixes the colors of paint, and a superb outdoor street scene of Dégas, filmed candidly. It is true that the cinema was still taking its first steps in 1915. It is to Guitry's credit that he handled the images in a fluid, well-conceived manner, capturing the essence of each artist in their natural manner."

The film is preserved in several archives around the world.

Jeanne Doré (1915)

Produced in France by Film d'Art; U.S. release by William F. Connor and Universal Film Company; Library of Congress Copyright 12-13-15149 prints; Directed by Louis Mercanton with Réné Hervil; Scenario by Louis Mercanton; Based on the stage play by Tristan Bernard; Length 1800 meters or five reels, about 60 minutes

Cast: Sarah Bernhardt as Jeanne Doré; Raymond Bernard as Jacques Doré; Mlle. Costa as Louise; Mlle. Seylor as Mme. Tissot

In 1900, Sarah starred in one of her greatest successes, *L'Aiglon* (The Eaglet), about the young son of Napoleon. The play was one of her biggest successes. A competitor made a film of *L'Aiglon* before she had withdrawn it from her theater's repertory. Bernhardt fought the film industry bitterly over this.

After the tragic loss of her leg, many people thought she would never work again. The movies had developed to a great degree in the few years since she had filmed Queen Elizabeth, and Jeanne Doré offered an opportunity to work in a manner that would obscure the loss of her limb. Sarah was shown standing as if to walk, when a cut to another person was arranged, and when the film again shifted to Sarah, it showed her at her destination. Other scenes were performed sitting at her desk in a library, standing on her feet as a courthouse witness, looking out of windows and kneeling at the bed of her son. By this time the film was kinder to her age and infirmity than the stage, and in this film she is still capable of moving us incredibly with her full-spread arms, her tragic hands and her joyous or stricken eyes.

Sarah Bernhardt had successfully done this play on the stage. She opened in the play in Paris in December 1913, followed by a profitable tour of the provinces in the early summer of 1914. The filming was done over a two-week period.

Jeanne Doré (1916). This stunning one-sheet poster was posted in front of theaters showing Sarah's first film since the amputation of her leg.

There is nothing very humorous about this morbid drama. It was a tale of a mother's love, not unlike *Madame X* and *Stella Dallas*. Sarah played the title role, a poor shopkeeper. Having been coerced into killing his stingy uncle by the woman he loves, a vamp, her son is condemned to death. In the final scene, Jeanne visits her son outside the prison cell on the eve of his execution. She comes to exchange a few final words with him. Because she has to communicate with him in the dark through the barred peephole of his door, the boy fails to recognize his mother. He thinks she is the faithless girl who has returned to him and pours out his love in a torrent of impassioned words, while the mother keeps silent and never disillusions him. As the stricken woman, Sarah was superbly poignant depicting this deceit to allow the son to go to his death reassured of the love he thought he had lost.

The making of the film is almost as dramatic as its script. In 1914, World War One was engulfing Europe, and the occupation of Paris seemed inevitable. Friends implored Sarah to get out of the city. An official from the war ministry called with a request that she leave the capital and take up residence in a safer part of the country. Sarah's name was on the list of hostages that the kaiser wanted brought to Berlin as soon as Paris fell. She decided to leave for Andernon-les-Bains in the Gironde.

Sarah had suffered since 1905 from a knee injury at a Rio de Janeiro theater during a stage fall. The injury had deteriorated to the extent that she could hardly walk. She had to sit with her leg stretched out before her, as by now, the doctors had resorted to the drastic therapy of immobilizing her entire limb in a plaster cast. She never recovered from the injury. Sarah was still touring in the play in early 1915, when her right leg

Jeanne Doré (1916). Sarah as the title character with Raymond Bernard as her son, Jacques. "In her eyes burned the fire that was lit at her son's birth, and would continue to burn as long as they both should live — a splendid flame of mother-love for her young."

developed gangrene from the old injury. In the bleak early morning of February 22, 1915, it was necessary to amputate the leg, and Sarah was confined to a wheelchair for months. Convalescence was long and difficult, and for a time, Madame Sarah's life hung in the balance. The leg had been removed high up on the thigh, almost at the hip, and the artificial contrivance that was provided had to be attached by means of a heavy girdle that fitted about her hips and stomach. Never in her life had she worn any sort of corset. After trying unsuccessfully to attach the cumbersome contraption by some other means, she flew into one of her old rages and ordered the thing to be thrown into the fire.

The public speculated as to how she would get about. The majority believed she would wear a wooden leg. Some thought she would depend upon crutches. She never made any attempt to try crutches, and the idea of a wheelchair filled her with contempt. Her solution was a specially designed litter chair with two horizontal shafts by which she could be carried about. Being Sarah Bernhardt, she dramatized the situa-

tion wherever she was carried, assuming the attitude of an empress in a procession.

If people had the idea that she was finished as an actress, she showed them her true spirit. Immediately upon leaving the hospital, she filmed *Jeanne Doré*. She could not yet walk on her new wooden leg, so she was shot either standing or sitting. This pinned her down and forced her to use facial expression rather than movement and helped her performance. The film got rave reviews and reflected well upon both its game star and the industry as an art form. Sarah oversaw every detail and now had an excellent sense of cinema. She appeared in over one hundred scenes, and because of her amputation, it was necessary for her to position herself strategically. She constantly instructed the company on cinematic deportment. Sarah found a distinct help in the use of real scenery in moving pictures. She enjoyed the brevity of each scene, which allowed the faculties to be "concentrated to a much higher degree than on a stage," she said. "Another feature about moving pictures which strikes me favorably is that once a scene has been acted and taken, repetition

Jeanne Doré (1916). Sarah as the title character, with Raymond Bernard as her son, Jacques. "I was born to be his mother. It is *being* his mother that has made life possible for me."

is unnecessary. After having repeated performances many hundreds of times in the theater, I find the variety and change of moving picture acting an excellent mental stimulant." While these comments were directed toward the projection of *Jeanne Doré*, they capture Sarah's basic attitudes toward the cinema as it existed in 1916. Raymond Bernard, son of the playwright Tristan Bernard, had made his stage debut opposite Sarah in the role of Jacques Doré and played the same role in the film. He observed that the film was made in two weeks.

H. H. Van Loan interviewed Sarah concerning this production. Her comments further substantiate the confidence that she had in the cinema as the dominant emerging art form. "The eye is the mirror of the brain, and the cinema has given to eye-play an infinitely greater scope, power, and importance. A true artist needs no audience to assist her art."

Jeanne Doré (1916). Jacques Doré demands money from his mother, Jeanne, to spend on gambling and a wicked woman who had fascinated him. She shrank instinctively from the blow this demand struck to her soul.

A review in *The New York Times*, October 18, 1915, heralded the headline: "Bernhardt in Photo Play. Her lameness hidden in *Jeanne Doré*, Shown Privately." The anonymous reviewer wrote

The first acting done by Sarah Bernhardt since the loss of one of her legs by amputation last summer was shown in motion pictures exhibited privately yesterday afternoon at the offices of the Universal Film Company in the Mecca Building. The film was a screen arrangement of Tristan Bernard's drama, "*Jeanne Doré*," and was taken in France.

It was in this play that Mme. Bernhardt was appearing in her theatre in Paris when the trouble with her leg forced her to leave the stage. Mme. Bernhardt's role is that of a middle aged woman, and while she ap-

pears a trifle older in the pictures, perhaps, than on her last visit here, she otherwise looks the same wonderful artiste of other years. Her great visual charm and her marvelous facial expression are still potent.

The film itself was so arranged before it was sent to this country that all evidences of the actress' lameness because of her artificial leg have been deleted. So the film, as it reached America, never shows the actress walking. In every scene in which she appears, she is shown either seated or standing.

The effect is no more confusing than in the average picture, which often baffles and irritates all but the incorrigible movie fan. The picture is so focused that the feet of the actress do not show, or if they do, only for short intervals, so there is nothing in the many scenes of the photodrama, which is melodramatic in the extreme, that

Jeanne Doré (1916). **Jeanne refuses all comfort from her neighbors as she agonizes over her son's arrest on charges of murder.**

would apprise the uninformed of her misfortune.

"According to the motion picture people, Mme. Bernhardt will never be able to act again on the legitimate stage," the directors who took the film so informed the company controlling the American rights. But William F. Connor, Mme. Bernhardt's American representative, denies this and insists that she will make her American tour this winter as planned. *Jeanne Doré* has been announced as one of the new offerings of her repertoire when she arrives. The picture, shown yesterday after further excisions and rearrangement, will be exhibited publicly within the month.

The Moving Picture World, October 16, 1915, wrote

Universal has just received a cablegram from its London headquarters that the negatives of *Jeanne Doré*, the Sarah Bernhardt production filmed in Europe, are on the way here, which is interesting, in view of the fact that the actress' personal tour has been twice postponed and may even be wholly abandoned.

Here we have once more a striking illusion of the amazing development of the motion picture art which has enabled the great

Frenchwoman to take just the precaution which will permit the millions of playgoers all over the world to pay her homage even if she never in the flesh faces the public again. The rumors that Madame Bernhardt was having trouble with her artificial leg need hardly be denied when it is stated, as the cables proclaim, that never in all her career has she entered into the spirit of an undertaking with more zest and less apparent fatigue than in the picturization of *Jeanne Doré*.

The extraordinary feature of this achievement is that not only will Bernhardt be seen in many cities and countries simultaneously, but for the first time in the history of stage or screen, a new play by a Parisian author of great renown will be seen on the screen before it is produced here as a spoken play.

Robert Grau wrote in "The Sarah Bernhardt of Today" in *Picture Play Magazine*,

"Seventy-one years young, the greatest actress of two centuries having successfully emerged from the operating table, is preparing for a final — so help me! — farewell to the land to which she came first three decades ago, and where she has ever been hailed as the world's greatest exponent of tragic roles.

Owing to the fact that Sarah Bernhardt is unable to secure the release of some of her players now serving at the front in France, the tour has been postponed for two months.

But even though the great French-woman may be forced to wholly abandon her tour of the legitimate theaters, even though Sarah never again can face the public here in the flesh, this generation of playgoers may take heart, for, thanks to the amazing development of a new art, and Madame's indomitable courage, the thousands of men and women who are bent upon paying her homage will be enabled to gaze upon the spectacle of the Bernhardt making the astonishing excursion from the operating table to the motion picture screen with all of her consummate grace and dignity."

Jeanne Doré (1916). **Jacques begs his mother for help as the police hunt for him.**

"I took this precaution," wrote Sarah to an American friend, "because after what I have sacrificed it would be truly a pity if this terrible war should, after all, perhaps force a postponement or even an abandonment of my tour, for, thanks to this heaven-born new art of the screen, I may still face my public in the very same roles."

Sarah Bernhardt is not new to the screen, but the Sarah of 1915, who rather than sacrifice her career, went courageously before the surgeons at Bordeaux and emerged there determined to resume her place as the foremost exponent of dramatic art, will be revealed on the magic screen not only to this generation of playgoers, but to future generations as well. Immediately after the announcement of Sarah's successful conquest of the knife, the great actress was bombarded with offers unparallel[ed] in the history of the theater."

A mighty film organization in New York City, with affiliations the world over, went into conferences behind closed doors with no other object in view than to entice the greatest actress of four generations into the domain of the camera man, so that all the world, no matter what happens, may enjoy her artistry on the screen for all time, even though the fates should interfere with her personal visit to these shores.

Public interest is just now greatest in seeing the Sarah of today, the Bernhardt with one leg. But which leg? No one really knows which, save Sarah, the doctors, and Madame's intimates. Certainly no one is granted any information.

The Moving Picture World, December 25, 1915, disclosed that Sarah was now partly an American because an artificial leg had been created by an American craftsman for her to add to her collection of twenty-four others. "The leg which Sarah Bernhardt wears in the Universal production of *Jeanne Doré* is an American model of 1915, according to the circumstantial account of its architect, John R. Clarke, who has just returned from Paris where he has an atelier

for artificial limbs. Mr. Clarke is an artist; he has temperament, and when he speaks of his work, his face brightens. He has but one leg of flesh and bone, and is fitted by experience for his vocation.

"With the member created from fabrics brought from this country and modeled by American craftsmen, the distinguished actress may be able to walk through the play of *Camille*, except in the last act; that is, as Mr. Clarke said today, if she practices sufficiently."

President Carl Laemmle, of the Universal Film Manufacturing Company, stated that in his opinion, "Mme. Bernhardt makes her last public appearance in the film

Jeanne Doré (1916). *Top:* The trial and conviction of Jacques Doré. *Left:* Jeanne goes to the prison to see her son on the last permissible visit, making the ultimate sacrifice, pretending that *she* is his sweetheart, just to have one more moment with him.

Jeanne Doré (1916). *Top:* Jeanne witnesses the execution, watching her son mount the steps to the guillotine. *Bottom, left:* Bluebird, the film's production company, provided a custom piano and orchestra score to accompany the film. *Bottom, right:* Musical cues on the sheet music noted scenes from the film to help the musicians synchronize their live playing with the projected film.

production of *Jeanne Doré*, the play in which she was appearing before her operation. But Mr. Clarke seems to think that such a wonderful woman, with muscles of wire and a will of iron, will be able to show the very spring of youth in her step. Now that she is partly American, he thinks she will again reveal the very goddess in her gait.

All the twenty-four other artificial legs in Mme. Bernhardt's wardrobe are French, and in that fair land of France the making of wooden legs is not yet an art."

The film is preserved in the archives of the Cinémathèque, Française in Paris, as well as in other archives.

Mères Françaises *(Mothers of France)* (1917)

Screenplay by Jean Richepin from his own play of the same name; Directed by Louis Mercanton and Réné Hervil; Film d'Art; U.S. Release as *Mothers of France* by World Films; Library of Congress copyrighted 210 prints

Cast: Sarah Bernhardt; Raymond Bernard; Louise Langrange; Berthe Jalabert; Gabriel Signoret; Jean Richepin

In late 1916, Sarah made this patriotic World War I film, the last film she fully completed, with the support of the French government. It is the only original screenplay in which she appeared, her other films all being adaptations of one of her stage plays.

In *Mothers of France*, she played the wife of a provincial squire living in the smooth and fertile fields of Meurcy, France. The tillers are gathering the harvest. The little village is wrapped in the tranquility of peace and plenty.

Monsieur and Madame D'Urbex are filled with happy excitement for young Robert D'Urbex, their only son, who has been made a lieutenant and is coming home that day to visit his family. The Lebron family, which includes father, mother, their daughter, Marie, and Nonet, an orphaned youth of nineteen, are managing the farm, which is a part of the D'Urbex estate. Guinot, the village schoolmaster, loves Marie, and a wedding has been arranged, although there is an unspoken tenderness between the girl and Nonet.

The tranquility of Meurcy is soon disturbed by news of diplomatic complications. War is imminent, and the call to mobilize comes suddenly. Nonet seizes a drum and strides through the village followed by an ever-increasing crowd. There is a passionate meeting in the square, and after it come scenes of soldiers parting from their loved ones. Nonet insists on going with the rest, although he is rejected as being under age.

Many months pass, and General D'Urbex is soon in command of the Champagne front. The regiment of Lieutenant D'Urbex has Victor Lebron as one of its corporals. The schoolmaster, Guinot, is a sergeant attached to the commissary department. Nonet is a soldier in the ranks.

Madame D'Urbex is a matron of the military hospital at Rheims. Her son, the lieutenant, leads a charge and is mortally wounded. He is taken to a field hospital where he remains awaiting death. When she learns of the imminent death of her son, Madam beseeches a friend to take her in one of the supply trucks to the place where she supposes the young lieutenant has been moved. It is a violation of military rules, but he consents. She plunges through the labyrinth of trenches searching for her son. At

Mères Françaises (*Mothers of France*) 1917. One-sheet poster from the European release (from the collection of Peter van der Waal).

last, when dawn is breaking, she finds him in a first-aid station, a shell-riddled building. He is stretched out upon a cot and at the final moment of life. He dies in her arms. She removes from his hand a letter he has scrawled, imploring her to overcome her grief and show herself a worthy example to the mothers of France. She devotes herself again to her duties as matron of the Rheims hospital, to which one day Guinot is brought, blinded for life. Beneath his pillow this sightless patient secrets the pocketbook of General D'Urbex. When fatally wounded by an exploding mine, the general had entrusted it to Guinot, who cannot bring himself to deliver this new blow to the heroic woman. The pocketbook remains under his pillow until Madame D'Urbex herself finds it there and learns the truth.

The doubly bereaved woman, sorely harassed but not utterly broken, resolves to devote herself to assuaging the grief of others. She goes back to her village to console the other stricken women. She is brave, hiding her feelings in public, and doing her part in the great work of healing torn bodies and lives. "We have not the right to curse," she tells her stricken neighbor, whose son has been blinded in battle. "Those for whom we weep are dead in order that our mother shall possess all things. France never dies."

Meanwhile, the schoolmaster, Guinot, has shown the manner of man he is by writing to the girl he loves that he cannot ask her to share the life of a sightless man and releasing her from her promise. Little Marie refuses to accept her liberty. Nonet comes home on leave, a medal on his breast, but he is unhappy because of the hopelessness of his love. After a scene with Marie, he determines to return to the trenches, but the schoolmaster overhears a part of the leave taking and reunites the young lovers.

Solitude weighs heavily on the blind man, who has sacrificed not only his eyesight, but put his heart upon the alter of duty. To him, the future seems empty indeed. Here again, Madame D'Urbex fills the breach. "Reflect," she says, "that there remains to you the members of a family for which you have a noble task to perform. Your pupils are waiting for you. To them you are no longer merely the schoolmaster, but a living example of the sacrifices we willingly make for our country."

These two proceed to the little schoolhouse, where Madame D'Urbex inscribes upon the blackboard this message: "So that the mothers shall no longer suffer, it is necessary that France carry on the war — war upon war — and that the glow of the future paradise shall illuminate itself from the bayonets of France."

The poet Jean Richepin, who also had a small part in the picture, wrote *Mères Françaises*, known in America as *Mothers of France*. In the film, Bernhardt, crippled and enfeebled, yet still the personification of Gallic emotion, sat through her scenes in a chair or stood propped against scenery. Much of the film was made near the front lines, in the towns of Challons and Rheims, and in trenches and field hospitals. In one scene, Sarah throws herself before a statue of Joan of Arc near the Cathedral of Rhiems, pleading with the saint to spare her family. The town gave the company only 15 minutes to film the scene, as the cathedral was sandbagged against shelling and had to be rewrapped immediately after filming.

Director Louis Mercanton told reporters, "Madame Bernhardt's perfect poise and calm during all the time in the trenches was to me an amazing exhibition of fortitude in a lady of her years (72), after a lifetime of luxury, pleasant surroundings, and at least the absence of physical peril." Throughout the making of the picture Sarah was accompanied by Mr. Mercanton, with whom the idea of the film originated and who actively superintended each step of its progress. He easily enlisted the interest of M. Richepin to write the drama. It was his love for the topic of his homeland and for the great Sarah Bernhardt as an artist that influenced him to enter the medium of photo plays. According to Mr. Mercanton, "Mme. Bernhardt spent six days at Challons, about fifteen miles from the German lines, and from this base was taken to the forward lines of trenches every day in a military automobile under the protection of two officers of the headquarters' staff.

"Upon two of these excursions she was actually under fire, and once she was treated to the spectacle of a German plane being shot down from the sky," he said. "This was so near she could distinctly hear the projectiles from the machine gun pelting against the foreign plane. We went on to Rheims, directly in the fighting zone, where extremely effective and dramatic episodes occur. One of these scenes shows the distracted wife and mother, before the still beautiful, though sadly lacerated, cathedral, offering a prayer at the base of the statue of Joan of Arc, her patron saint and the patron saint of France, for her country and her loved ones."

In *The Moving Picture World*, February 10, 1917, Louis Mercanton found keen competition in this country as he tried to dispose of the rights to market the film in America and Canada. The French government was part owner, having arranged and assisted in the war scenes, and unified the intense national spirit at the bottom of the undertaking. Mercanton concluded negotiations and departed without making a distribution deal for the unusual reason that competition for the rights was so strong as to make it advisable for him to consult fur-

Mothers of France (1917) featured Sarah as Madame D'Urbex. In this frame enlargement from the film, Sarah performed at the actual front lines of battle in France during World War I.

ther with his associates prior to taking final action. Before leaving on January 17, 1917, he said to a reporter

To tell the truth, my departure is somewhat in the nature of a retreat. When I came to New York to arrange for the photo drama here, I had no idea of what was to happen. My supposition was that I should arrange the details in the ordinary course of business, sign the necessary contracts and go my way in peace. The process was taken out of my hands. ... For two or three days I talked with the representatives of the distributors and it early became apparent that I had underestimated the possibilities of our photoplay. The competition for *Mothers of France* is very far beyond anything I had anticipated, and I am determined to avoid committing our company in too much haste. If this were a merely commercial enterprise, the decision would be simple enough.

My film, *Mothers of France,* is epochal in

Mothers of France (1917) *Top:* Sarah was featured as Madame D'Urbex beseeching the local authorities for help for the women of her homeland. *Bottom:* Sarah in a scene with the full cast.

a number of ways. In the first place Mme. Bernhardt is its star. In the second, it was written by M. Jean Richepin, poet, dramatist and member of the French Academy. And finally, it was photographed in the trenches by arrangement and with the assistance of the government. This play will be a part of the official record of the present European war, and will be preserved through the generations. The authorities in

France, civil and military, are deeply interested in it for it carries to the world a genuine representation of France as it is, not merely Paris, with which most persons are familiar, but that provincial France of which the outside world knows little or nothing.

M. Richepin, as doubtless you are not aware, is the mayor of the little town in which he resides. He knows and loves the atmosphere of the local life. Through this condition, he has been able to im-

In *Mothers of France* (1917), Madame D'Urbex says to her neighbor's son, blinded in battle, "Reflect that there remains to you the members of a family for which you have a noble task to perform. Your pupils are waiting for you. To them you are no longer merely the schoolmaster, but a living example of the sacrifices we willingly make for our country."

part to the opening scenes of his play, the precise effect of the war declaration upon the people who are the backbone of France, and to interpret the lofty, holy patriotism with which they entered upon a task which called from them the last ounce of self-sacrifice, grief and suffering."

Audiences and critics, too, were bowled over by the blatant but effective propaganda film. "Actress at her best," "thrilling war film," said various reviews. Burns Mantle wrote that "most of it you see through a mist of tears."

A review in Variety, March 16, 1917, said about *Mothers of France*,

In spite of the inclement weather, the Rialto was packed Sunday afternoon with picture fans anxious to witness the American premiere of the Eclipse Company's film production of Jean Richepin's *Mothers of France*, with Sarah Bernhardt as the star, and directed by Louis Mercanton. They were well repaid for their trouble, for they saw a fine visualization of life in France during these troublous times, admirably acted

by a company of screen artists and with wonderfully clear photography. There is no attempt at "comedy relief," merely a depiction of the sufferings of the natives, both rich and poor, and the ravages of war, sparing none. The perennial Bernhardt is as virile as ever. The picture is ingeniously "cut" at just the moments when she is about to walk or has just moved from one spot to another, and to one unfamiliar with the fact that she lost a leg, the thought would never suggest itself that she never indulges in pedestrianism. She doesn't look over fifty, and is today as great an artiste as she ever was.

A review in *The New York Times*, March 12, 1917, proclaimed the headline, "Sarah Bernhardt in Real War Film," "*Mothers of France* from Scenario of Jean Richepin moves Rialto audience," "Triumph for the Actress." "Camera Shows Her in Hospitals, Camps, and the very Trenches with the Poilus." The *Times* review said the following:

Mothers of France, a cinematic epic of the great war, is the photo-drama for which

While filming *Mothers of France*, Sarah was carried to the film site on a litter borne by volunteer soldiers. Several times during the filming she was within hearing of the actual bombardments.

Sarah Bernhardt acted before she sailed from France to come to America last fall. Jean Richepin, dramatist and academician, wrote the scenario, and the French Government offered every facility for enacting its scenes before a truly martial background. It was exhibited here for the first time yesterday at the Rialto.

Mothers of France atones for most of the sins of the movies. To see it is recompense for having sat through a series of atrocious and banal war films purporting to point [out] a moral. It is propaganda, subtle and powerful, that must move even the most callused and neutral observer. Only the pro-Teuton could see it and not be touched by its sincerity and its art — the art that is inherent in truth. It is a brief for the women of France who are doing their bit behind fighting lines, told in terms of the most vivid realism. The story unfolded is of the sacrifices of a small group of neighbors in a village of France. It is a tale whose various details have been duplicated in every corner of that fair land since the war began.

A nation at war provided the "mise en scene" for this universal drama of France, and that nation's greatest actress gave her services that the world might weep with the mothers of France and rejoice at their courage of spirit; a courage that passes all understanding. Mme. Bernhardt acted the role

of the central figure of the story, a choice that was ideal because of her art. More than any other living person she typifies to America the joy, the warmth, the strength, and the capacity to drink to the full of life that is France.

The power of the movies to obliterate space removes the handicap of her inability to walk freely; she is always revealed standing or sitting, and one is conscious only of the wonderful expressiveness of her countenance and gestures. In one scene in particular, in which she stands before the portrait of her dead husband, the poignancy of the grief expressed seems to lose nothing through its inarticulateness.

The skill of the players, including the children, all of whom, possess the Gaelic [*sic*] felicity of gesture, combined with the unmistakable veracity of the scenes to stir the emotions. Mme. Bernhardt, in the role of the mother, is pictured in the hospitals, the commissary camps, and even in the very trenches with the Poilus. Once she is shown waiting in the corner of a transverse to allow a squad of soldiers to run by, each carrying an aerial torpedo.

Again she stands before the statue of Joan of Arc in front of the war-scarred Cathedral of Rheims, its shattered windows and bag-protected buttresses plainly visible. Real chateaux, real peasant women toiling in the fields, and real munitions smoke give a flavor that no amount of paint and plaster villages and trenches filled with tin soldiers hired at a dollar a day could ever hope to approximate.

The artistic value of the film itself has been enhanced by the manner of exhibition. The singing of the "Marseilles" [*sic*] precedes the showing, and throughout its course, appropriate music, with the French national anthem as the recurrent theme, is played. Then by the process of double projection, glimpses of Geraldine Farrar's por-

Mothers of France (1917) had one scene with Sarah in front of the statue of Joan of Arc at Rheims Cathedral. The shelling during the actual World War I battlements was halted for fifteen minutes and the cathedral buttressed with sandbags so this one moment could be photographed for the film.

trayal of Joan of Arc are thrown on the screen synchronously with the other picture.

The film is preserved in the archives of the Cinémathèque, Française in Paris.

It Happened in Paris (1919)

Presenter: Madame Sarah Bernhardt; Supervisor: Madame Sarah Bernhardt; Directed by David Hartford; Scenarist: Jack Cunningham; Story: Madame Sarah Bernhardt; Scenarist Editor: Winifred Dunn; Camera: M. Matzene; Tyrad Pictures Inc., Distribution Co.; States rights release, Dec. 26, 1919.; 5 reels, with a running time of 55 minutes.

Cast: Sarah Bernhardt as Herself; Madame Yorska as Juliette/Yvonne Dupré; W. Lawson Butt as Romildo, the Gypsy; Rose Dione as Creota; Charles Gunn as Dick Gray; Hayward Mack as Léon Naisson; David Hartford as Himself

The film was shot at the Brunton studios in Los Angeles. Madame Benhardt is shown in a prologue discussing scenes with Madame Yorska, her protégée, and director David Hartford.

In *The Exhibitors Trade Review*, November 22, 1919, Helen Rockwell wrote, "No less a person than Madame Sarah Bernhardt is credited with having written the photoplay as a means of introducing her protégé [*sic*], Mme. Yorska, to the film fans of America. It often happens that a great artist who is able to conquer one art, is unable and unfit to conquer them all, and it will be much pleasanter to remember Mme. Bernhardt as the world's greatest tragedienne than as the author of this picture."

This cheerless story deals with both the underworld and the high society of Paris. The story focuses on Yvonne Dupré, the sole survivor of a once-noble French family, who makes a modest living selling her paintings to Léon Naisson. Unknown to her, Léon resells the paintings for exorbitant prices, claiming them to be the work of a famous artist.

Léon confides to Romildo, one of Yvonne's gypsy models, that he is strongly attracted to Yvonne, but that she had rejected him. Romildo's lover is Juliette, a fiery Apache dancer, who bears a strong resemblance to Yvonne. Romildo drugs Juli-

ette and delivers her, for one thousand dollars, to Léon, who rapes Juliette in her sleep. Léon soon discovers she is not Yvonne. He then plots to have Yvonne's American sweetheart, Dick Gray, see them together, causing Gray to upbraid the baffled Yvonne. Léon then plants some forged papers in Yvonne's studio and tips off the police, who are closing in on her operation. After Yvonne's arrest, her foster sister tells Juliette that she was stolen by gypsies as a child and is really Yvonne's twin sister. After Juliette exposes Léon, Yvonne and Dick are reunited.

In *Motion Picture News*, November 22, 1919, an anonymous reviewer wrote, "Mme. Yorska, a protégé [*sic*] of Sarah Bernhardt, is in a dual role and proves that she is an actress of ability. As Juliette, the dancer, she is fiery and untamable, and as the sister she portrays the artistic girl born of wealth but forced to make her art pay as she has been reduced in finances by the death of her father."

In the Sunday, March 7, 1920, issue of *Wid's Daily*, a motion picture trade publication, the film's credits are annotated with the following remarks:

Cameraman: Not credited

As a Whole: Picture hurt by several bad cuts; a good story but with one fairly raw situation; best suitable for transient and downtown houses.

Story: A dual-role story well worked out in the main.

Direction: Generally good, sometimes stagey.

Photography: Good

Lighting: Effective

Star: Is a mighty fine actress, but lacks physical appeal.

Support: Lawson Butt heads good cast.

Exteriors: Paris street setting among few used.

Length of Production: about 5,000 ft.

Further comments from the same publication state,

Under the sensational title of *It Happened in Paris*, Mme. Yorska, known as Sarah Bernhardt's understudy and protégée, is presented in a story said to have been written by the famed actress herself. There are faults to find with the picture for, aside from containing one fairly risqué situation, the influence of which is felt throughout the entire story, the production was injured in the cutting, and the star, while full of expression tempered with restraint, has none of the physical or beauty appeal that makes for picture popularity here.

The picture shows marks of extensive editing and even altering of the original course of the story. This is obvious two or three times to the discredit of the continuity of the action. Mme. Yorska is a real actress and her emotional range omits no expression. She is not good looking, but certainly overcomes this handicap to a certain extent by her fine performance.

In the *Exhibitors Trade Review*, Helen Rockwell remarked, "Mme.

It Happened in Paris (1919). This advertising poster featured Sarah in the artwork. She was the "presenter" and "supervisor" of the film directed by David Hartford, and she appeared in a prologue discussing the film with her protégée and understudy Madame Yorska.

Yorska favors the violent style of acting and in top-most scenes is entirely unsuppressed. She is ably assisted by an intelligent company of players." The trade journal further encouraged theater owners to "Get the Parisian atmosphere in your theater and lobby. Dress your attendants in the costume of Paris Apaches. If possible, secure a large portrait of Sarah Bernhardt and place it in the lobby with an appropriate announcement stating that this is her first venture as an author."

The film appears not to have been preserved.

Daniel (1921)

Based on the play *Daniel* by Louis Verneuil; Produced by Pathé Gazette.

On November 9, 1920, Sarah Bernhardt announced that she would appear in a full-length play called *Daniel*, by Louis Verneuil. Sarah's character was not in the first two acts of the play but appeared in the last two as a thirty-ish morphine addict with a noble heart. It is a story of two brothers who have loved the same girl. The older brother has won, marries her, and Daniel, the younger brother, has degenerated into a slow death of seclusion and narcotics. The play ran for many months, was a resounding success, and went on a lengthy tour.

Rouben Mamoulian, acclaimed director of motion pictures, recalled seeing Sarah in the play *Daniel*:

> I went to the theater early. The auditorium was already crowded; a few more minutes and the house was full. The legend of Sarah Bernhardt seemed to glow and vibrate in the air, to give the house a quickened pulse of excitement. The crystal chandelier, the lights, the orange and gold upholstery of the seats, the eyes of the people, all seemed brighter and more festive than usual. Also, the theater was much nosier. Everybody was talking, even strangers were conversing with each other. A buzzing beehive awaiting the arrival of the queen bee! It seemed strange

In the stage play of *Daniel* (1921) Sarah played a dying morphine addict.

Pathé News poster advertising the newsreel cameramen who recorded outstanding events of the day, including Sarah Bernhardt in *Daniel* (1921).

how prescient an audience is. The great success of a play really begins before the curtain goes up. And what is even more amazing, the quality of this excitement is never quite the same; it borrows its accents and colors from the quality of the performance to come. Everybody knew about the great artist's loss of one leg, her advanced age and the brittle porcelain mask on her face to take care of the wrinkles.

Then suddenly through the din of noises came the knocking of the wooden mallet on the floor backstage, the strange and rather prosaic signal the French use to announce the curtain. The great moment had arrived and the lights began to dim. There on the stage, reclining on many pillows in bed, was Sarah Bernhardt. The house shook under the strain of the ovation for the artist. Bernhardt bent her curly yellow head low, accepting the tribute with regal grace and dignity. The applause was interspersed with shouts of "Sarah! La divine Sarah!" The clatter went on a long time before it died out; people obviously were enjoying giving vent to their feelings. After that, the performance went on.

I watched Bernhardt with utter concentration. I did not want to miss anything. I had two dominant feelings throughout the performance; one was avid curiosity, and the other a sense of the legend of Bernhardt persistently hovering in the back of my mind, the constant realization that I was looking at someone who had been very great, very glamorous in the past. This was never obliterated by a reaction to how wonderful she was now, not in memory but in the actual present. She looked thin and small. She was very old, I thought — much older than I expected. The mass of curly yellow hair looked like an embarrassing and incongruous apology of an old woman for her age. The face looked like a porcelain mask. She could hardly smile, and one had a feeling that the smile hurt her parched pink and white face. I listened to her voice, the famous "golden voice" that had enchanted thousands. The spell was not there now, except the spell of past glory, which also is strong and hard to resist. The voice was very old and a little raspy; it almost frightened me at first, but later I grew used

to it, and before long I found it fascinating and attractive. The "r" of every Parisian is an outstanding guttural sound. Hers was even more so — it started deep in her throat and rolled many times over her tongue before coming out to strike the ear, like the roll of a very old, yet sonorous snare drum.

I especially remember the line she addressed to the actor playing a doctor, offering him cigarettes with a crisply graceful gesture: "Cigarrrrrettes, Docteurrre?" For a long time after the performance I used to repeat that line to myself, as I sometimes do even now when thinking of Bernhardt. It brings her back vividly to my mind. If death were to assume a woman's shape and were to offer you a cigarette, that is the way she would sound, I'm sure; dry buckshot rolling on parchment. I noticed the unusual way she held a cigarette in her right hand — the hand clenched into a fist, the cigarette between the first finger and the other three, the lip-end supported by the thumb from underneath.

I was watching the performance with absorbed concentration, waiting for that little touch, that *quelque chose* that makes greatness. Actors of genius might go through a performance which is fine and deeply satisfactory, but still within the range of merely talented performing. Then suddenly in one scene, or in one gesture or intonation, they will do something that is in the nature of a revelation, a sign of genius. Then for an inspired moment the stage becomes illuminated by the great presence, like a black landscape that comes to life under the swift, blinding whip of lightning. Bernhardt did this at the end of the play in the death scene. Propped with pillows, in bed, she was dying. In the last few seconds, while the stream of life was still flowing through her heart, she sat up straight. Suddenly something strange and powerful crept into her voice and into the face, in spite of the blank, doll-like mask of enamel that covered it. A few more half-whispered words and life was no more.

Now, I'm sure any other actress dying in this particular scene would have fallen back onto the pillows, her arms gracefully at her sides, her face pale against the frame of curly hair, lying on the pillows for the whole au-

In the film *Daniel* (1921), Sarah played a dyring morphine addict asking to have a letter from his love read to him. Without the use of spoken dialogue, the film substituted a subtitle insert preceding this enlargement from the actual film: "My eyes grow dim. ... Read it to me before I go."

dience to see, with its last smile of radiance, serenity, sadness or what have you. Not so with Bernhardt. Unexpectedly, with a shock that made you sit up and quiver in your chair, she fell forward, like a figure of lead, heavy and limp, her arms collapsing pathetically and awkwardly at her side, palms up. She moved no more. There was death — stark, final, unpremeditated. Seemingly so, of course — but that was high art. That was the one touch that proclaimed: Sarah Bernhardt the great is on that stage! The house rocked with an immediate fury of applause. People were jumping up and down on their seats. There were many curtain calls. Her bows were beautifully prearranged. She stood in the middle of the stage, her arms outstretched horizontally supported by two actors, her head bowed low — a complete image of Christ on the Cross. She did not change the position through all the curtain

calls, except occasionally to lift her head and then to droop it again on her chest. I have never heard so much noise in the theater. I joined in the general tumult by applauding until my hands hurt, and yelling lustily at the top of my voice.

At the age of seventy-seven, Sarah filmed this play, at least in part, as a silent movie. All that seems to remain is the final scene, in which Sarah's character dies. It is uncertain at this time if this was one scene from a full-length film, or if it is the only scene that was filmed. It was distributed as part of "Pathe Gazette," the name of an early Pathe newsreel service. The film lay unseen for eighty years until the research for this book unearthed the lost footage buried among scraps of film in an obscure archive.

In this frame enlargement from the film *Daniel*, Sarah played one of her famous death scenes. This close-up is from the moment when death overtakes the sickened morphine addict.

The film opens with a full view of the bedroom in the home of Daniel. He is in bed, dying. Two titles follow: "Daniel: a tale of the Eternal Triangle and a man's self-sacrifice" and "Neglected and forlorn Genevieve, wife of Daniel's brother, a man whose God is money, has fled with another and Daniel, with self-sacrifice, has taken the blame." In a long shot, Daniel, played by Sarah, is at death's door. He tells his old friend the doctor how his brother unjustly suspected him of complicity in Genevieve's flight. A companion approaches the sickbed while another man holds Daniel's hand. A conversation takes place between Daniel and the man who sits beside her bed. She throws up her hand. The film cuts to a close-up of the doctor. There follows a title card, "Daniel, I have sent for your brother....

He must see you at once." The film cuts back to a close-up of the doctor.

A servant comes into the room with a cup of tea, but Daniel sends him away. He drinks from a glass of medicine instead. There follows a grotesque close-up of Sarah as Daniel. She clutches at her heart and looks distressed. As she begins to speak, a title card pronounces, "I helped Genevieve because I loved her. She was miserable and I so wanted to see her happy, even with another, before I died." Daniel's brother considers his words, while the other man sits and glares at the two of them.

Daniel throws up his arms in a wide gesture of despair. He puts his hand on his heart and implores her brother for forgiveness. In a medium shot, he begs the brother for forgiveness. The brother eventually suc-

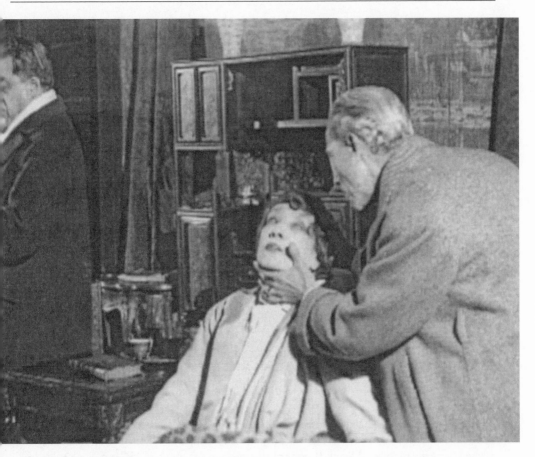

In this frame enlargement from the film *Daniel*, Sarah is seen dead in a garish close-up, gripped in the hands of her doctor.

cumbs and they embrace. Daniel holds his head and cries. The brother sits heavily in a chair and wipes his eyes. The other man rushes to the bedside. In a title Daniel declaims, "Albert, I had a letter from her this morning. She says she is happy at last." Daniel holds the letter in his hand, then gives it to his brother, saying "My eyes grow dim. Read it to me before I go."

Albert stands and reads the letter. In a close-up of the letter the script is in French, and dissolves into English. The text reads, "My dear Daniel, the words I write express my eternal gratitude to you, dear friend, for helping my love and myself enter that paradise of joy I dreamed of, but alas, never saw during the past two unhappy years. Your noble, self-sacrifice must...." The

brother continuing to read the letter as Daniel makes a melodramatic gesture, then collapses.

The first man tries to revive him, but he is dead. He pulls Sarah's head back in a garish close-up, showing the face of Daniel with eyes closed. A title card pronounces, "But there was no ending for Daniel. The gates had opened wide and his soul had passed beyond." In a close-up, the brother looks shocked, and falls to his knees. With a final title card the film concludes, "The End."

The film seems to be a reproduction of the stage play, but it is cut into a definite cinematic form in the style of silent movies of the era. Careful lighting is apparent, and it is obvious that some care was taken in the

But there was no ending for Daniel.... the gates had opened wide and his soul had passed beyond.

In this frame enlargement from the film *Daniel*, the final subtitle concludes the tragic story.

production. This existing five-minute segment of the film is all that remains of one of the last performances of Sarah Bernhardt, but it is like a gold nugget discovered after many days of panning in the dirt for treasure. For many years this piece of film has been lost, buried in a few film archives under reams of unrelated documentary footage of the actress. Recently rediscovered,

the film is an indelible record of her unquestionable brilliance. It is a document of an actress who was old and courageous, still mistress of a fine technique, but burnt to cold ashes, tired; an actress who was once great, and who still found strength and valor to tread the wooden planks behind the footlights which she loved so well.

La Voyante
(The Fortune Teller) (1923)

Directed by Louis Mercanton; Written by Sacha Guitry from a play of the same name; Photographed by Raymond Agnel and Alphonse Gibory

Cast: Sarah Bernhardt; Mary Marquet; Sacha Guitry; Harry Baur; Lili Damita; George Melchoir; François Fratellini; Mme. Pâquerette; Raymond Agnel; Alphonse Gibory; Jeanne Brindeau (Stand-in for Mme. Bernhardt)

La Voyante was Sarah's final performance, at the age of 78. The making of this film is one of the most poignant examples

of indomitable courage in the history of the motion picture industry. Filming began in March of 1923. Although extremely ill,

Sarah had risen from her bed to act once more. There were debts to be paid. It was impossible for her to go back to the theater, and films were the only solution. Leon Abrams, the American, started work on *La Voyante* in Bernhardt's home.

Cornelia Otis Skinner wrote in her book, *Madame Sarah*, "In the autumn of 1922 she collapsed into a coma which lasted about an hour and was unable to go on the night of the dress rehearsal for *Un Sujet de Roman*, in which she was to appear with Sacha Guitry. The opening was postponed, and for a month she lay in bed desperately ill. All at once she took a marked turn for the better, and it was with characteristic zest that she agreed to take part in a film Sacha Guitry was about to make for a Hollywood company. This was something called *La Voyante*, in which she was cast as a clairvoyant who foretells the future. As she was still too ill to work in a studio, it was decided to shoot her scenes in her house. Scenery, klieg lights and photographic equipment were installed and she set to work."

Basil Woon in *The Real Sarah Bernhardt Whom Her Audiences Never Knew* quoted Mme. Pierre Berton, "I was among those who called at the little house in the Boulevard Pereire on the night of December 31, when it was thought that she must die. But she rallied, and though all her friends and she herself knew that it was but a temporary reprieve, she insisted on going back to work. Not this time, on the stage, but in her own house before the motion-picture camera.

"A syndicate organized by a young American in Paris and directed by another American, Leon Abrams, made her an offer of, I think it was, 5,000 francs per day. She was, as usual, penniless, and the offer was a godsend."

She posed for the film, with her chimpanzee, in the studio at the rear of her house. So needy was she that, just before lapsing into unconsciousness for the last

These photographs appeared in a collage in the June 1923 issue of *Le Théâtre et Comédie Illustré*. The top photograph shows a scene being staged within rooms inside Sarah's home. The second photograph is Sarah watching the arrangements in progress. The middle photograph shows the film crew setting up a shot. The bottom photograph shows Sarah in conference with the film director, Louis Mercanton.

time, she demanded that the moving-picture men should be admitted to the bedroom. "They can film me in bed," she said, her voice scarcely audible, so weak was she. "Now, don't object," as Professor Vidal remonstrated, "they pay me 5,000 franc each time I pose!"

A backcloth of Paris was placed in the room, and the company continued against the wishes of all but the magnificent and heroic Bernhardt.

Her eyes were so weakened by the spreading poison in her system that she had to wear dark glasses between takes. A few frames of this film reveal a corpselike figure bent over tarot cards, the effect heightened by the kohl beneath her eyes.

In *Le Cinéma* of September 1927, an unknown reviewer wrote, "There is in Paris an unfinished motion picture called *La Voyante*. It is not a very wonderful production, and would not have been had it been completed. But in it appears a familiar face — the face of an aged actress, who, acclaimed the greatest feminine figure of the contemporary theatre, was enacting her last role. It was often said of Sarah Bernhardt that she was immortal. In an earlier age, however, only her fame would have been deathless. The memory of man is short, and her beloved theatre could not preserve her presence. But she is immortal, and through an agency to which she was apathetic. In *La Voyante* one can see the last gestures of the princess of gestures."

In an article called "The Last Role of Sarah Bernhardt" in *Pictureplay*, November 1923, Daphne Carr wrote,

At her age! And I have never seen her act better," said a great actor, his eyes dimmed with tears, of Madame Sarah Bernhardt but a few days before her death.

The incident took place in Madame Bernhardt's home on the Boulevard Periere. The actor was Harry Baur, who had been personally chosen by Madame Bernhardt to take a leading role in the motion picture, which she considered her last gift to the world.

Plans for the picture had been evolving during one of Madame Bernhardt's periods of frail health. At last her doctors said that she was strong enough to play, and her own determination prevailed. She would create the role. "*Quand même,*" her motto of

"Through it all" was not to be dropped because of age or ill health. To prevent unnecessary fatigue the working studio was arranged in her own house. Her famous conservatory was transformed from a veritable treasure house of objets d'art into a typical Montmartre living room, the home of an aged clairvoyant. Where priceless paintings and rich cloth of gray and gold once covered the walls, a surface, bare except for ordinary wallpaper and a few simple prints, was visible. Where a handsome carved table, the gift of a European monarch, had stood, an inexpensive and serviceable table took its place. But for the battery of arc and mercury lights, the uninitiated visitor might have fancied himself in the room of a modest scholar, and at the same time would have been impressed by the sense that a strange and wonderful personality inhabited the room.

"I saw Madame Bernhardt when she was carried into the studio on a sort of improvised palanquin for her first session before the camera," said Harry Baur. "Bonjour, Messieurs," she said, and with an inimitable gesture, she caused an abrupt silence in the little group of assistants.

Proud and smiling, in spite of infirmity, she was carried in as only royalty is carried, the bearers four servants who had remained with her through the triumphs and troubles of years. A dozen arms reached for the honor of helping to lower the palanquin. In the midst of an awe-struck silence she was placed in her chair behind the *Clairvoyant's* table.

The mercury lights sputtered. Spotlights played in a weird way from concealed locations. Every one was ill at ease with the exception of Madame Bernhardt, who at once interested herself in the technical end of the arrangements, seemingly oblivious to the profound impression that her personality produced on us. To avoid any sacrifice of the great actress' strength, work was immediately begun. Cameras and lights were trained on her. In the midst of a superb gesture she suddenly stopped, and with a gracious smile demanded Jacqueline. Who was Jaqueline? The director remembered. He snapped his fingers and a trained monkey, which, in the play, takes the part of the clairvoyant's servant and pet, appeared. A slight motion of Madame Bernhardt's hand and Jaqueline leaped to her lap. From somewhere the great artiste produced two crackers and a banana. While Jacqueline nibbled these delicacies the battery of mercury light, baby spot lights, attendant electricians, camera men and the director waited for Madame Bernhardt to establish an *entente cordiale* with the monkey who was to appear with her in her last role more constantly than any human actor.

Work was resumed. The director said, "Ready." Lights concentrated. For a moment the great actress, now so frail, rested. Her trembling hands steadied against her face, her elbows on the table. Her eyes, for the moment expressionless, looked straight ahead. Slowly something occurred — we knew not what — but the room was filled with a new personality. My throat tightened and the director, standing in front of me, pulled at his collar. Her eyes now had a look of infinite understanding; her hands moved in unbroken gestures, the fingers now steady. It was no longer Sarah Bernhardt but the character of her last role, *La Voyante*, who was before us. For six minutes she continued to be the profound medium. "Scene finished," said the director huskily.

Instantly, *La Voyante* disappeared. Madame Bernhardt's hands shook. Her eyes closed against the glare of the lights, and she dropped her head limply in her hands. The director hastened to her with a pair of dark glasses, turned away and wiped his eyes. An old electrician drew his wrist across his cheek, and a young assistant openly brought out his handkerchief. Madame Bernhardt's secretary hurried to her with a glass of brandy, and both she and the director advised that work be stopped for the day. The Bernhardt shook her head. She sipped her glass of brandy.

"I am not tired. We will presently begin the next scene." Madame Bernhardt was used to commanding.

And it was in this intense atmosphere, acting against these difficulties, that the combined efforts of this greatest tragedienne and the director produced and recorded her last role of the clairvoyant

La Voyante (1923). One of the last moments of her life, between takes of the film shot in a studio set up in her home, her eyes weakened by the uremia poison spreading through her body, protected from the hot lights by dark glasses.

who, in time of peril, influenced the destinies of France to a happy conclusion.

Cast member Mary Marquet recalled, "There was nothing left of her. All at once the director shouted 'Camera!' Sarah rose from her torpor; her face lit up, her neck grew longer, her eyes shone. 'What do I do?' she demanded in a voice that was young and strong. We were all stupefied. She had just dropped thirty years."

The choice of her supporting cast shows the great discrimination exercised by Madame Bernhardt. It includes Harry Baur, who has often acted with Madame Bernhardt, Marie Marquet, a gifted actress of the Comédie Française, George Melchior, the foremost juvenile lead of the French screen, and Lili Damita, winner of a recent beauty prize of France.

With this distinguished cast Madame Bernhardt played out her marvelous interpretation of a character who used her gift of second sight to illuminate the problems of life for all those who came in contact with her.

Perfect artist to the last, the Divine Sarah overcame seemingly insurmountable difficulties to realize her last role and bequeath a priceless legacy to the world.

Those were heroic weeks. A studio was set up in her rooms, tangles of spotlights and bunch lights impeded the scurrying of electricians and scene builders. Harry Baur, Lili Damita, Mary Marquet, George Melchior, and others supported the star. Cameras ground, and the story was well under

This still photograph, shot between takes of *La Voyante* (1923), shows Sarah only hours before her death, valiantly playing her last scene.

way when Bernhardt was carried to bed again. It was typical of her that she wanted to select another actress to take her place, that the film might be finished.

According to Mme. Pierre Berton, "Her insistence on fulfilling her contract to play in this cinema play, was, according to the doctors, the cause of her last collapse. It was more than her strength could stand. She was really dying when she faced the camera on the last two occasions. But her indomitable will triumphed over her body almost to the last, and, until the dreadful malady paralyzed her, she continued acting. My tears are falling as I write these last lines. They are difficult sentences to fashion. I am no poet, and words could not add to the drama of that night when the divine call-boy came for Sarah Bernhardt."

On the following day it was no longer possible to continue filming. It was spring in Paris and Sarah asked her son, Maurice, to cover her with roses, lilacs and Parma violets.

A priest was brought to administer the last rites, and at five past eight on the evening of March 26, Sarah's life-long dream was realized "to become a legend during my lifetime, and not to be dead before dying."

She died before her part was completed. The film was finished using a stand-in playing Sarah's remaining scenes with her back to the camera.

On her tomb in Père Lachaise Cemetery are graven the two words with which she directed her life to the last, the words which represent the determination that made possible this last role, "Quand Même."

The true glory of Bernhardt cannot be judged from her films. Rene Clair has used her as an illustration of the fact that "the theatre is one thing and the cinema another. Bernhardt never troubled herself to learn the laws of screen technique. Her attitudes were unsuited to the newer art and her voice was mute. Her films," he declared, "are documents and not works."

She is an important factor in the history of the screen. And her stage work is preserved in only one form — little round reels of film.

Author's Note

The films of Sarah Bernhardt have lain on dusty archives shelves hidden from view for most of a hundred years. *Adrienne Lecouvreur* and *It Happened in Paris* appear to have even been lost forever. Only *Queen Elizabeth* has been in wide distribution in 35mm, 16mm, 8mm, and VHS from a wide variety of distributors. Given the interest in Sarah's plays and silent movies in general, it is astounding that none of those holding the existing prints of her other motion pictures have taken the time to clean them up for the enjoyment of a new, younger audience. They deserve to be transferred digitally onto playable formats, cleaned of blemishes, restored to the careful tints and tones used in their original release, and scored for proper presentation. The motion picture industry that owes so much to the pioneering spirit of the theater's foremost actress has shown a remarkable lack of interest in making her films available to the audiences of today.

La Tosca is said to be hidden at Le Cinémathèque Gaumont archives as well as at others; *Sarah Bernhardt à Belle Isle* is preserved by the UCLA archives and at other institutions; Pathé Archives and the WPA Film Library have the footage from *Daniel* available only on individual request at a steep price; *Mères Françaises* is known to be collecting dust at the Centre National de la Cinématographe in France and with the Swedish Film Archive in Stockholm; *La Dame Aux Camélias* is buried in the Museum of Modern Art in New York; *Le Duel de Hamlet* is isolated in stillness at the German Kinemathek in Berlin and elsewhere; *Jeanne Doré*, *La Voyante* and almost all of the other titles are said to be held captive in the darkness of the vaults at the Cinémathèque Française in Paris. None of these are allowed to be viewed by general audiences.

Fortunately, the recording industry has had a number of copies of Sarah's recordings available for years on 33rpm LP albums for the study and wonder of Sarah's admirers.

"Came the dawn" was a title card used excessively in early silent movies. As we move toward the one-hundredth anniversary of the making of Sarah's first actual dramatic film, *La Tosca*, it is my hope that "come the dawn" of 2010 the world will again have the joy of watching our greatest actress seemingly alive in new releases of her films.

"I depend on these films for my immortality," Sarah said. Will the new generation of audiences give immortality to her?

Appendix: Chronological Listing of Plays, Films, and Recordings Performed by Sarah Bernhardt

(Revivals and one-time special performances are not listed.)

At the Comédie Française

1862 Iphigénie
Valérie
Les Femmes Savantes
L'Etourdi

At the Gymnase

1864 Le Père de la Débutante
Le Démon du Jeu
Un Soufflet n'est Jamais Perdu
La Maison sans Enfants
Le Etourneau
Le Premier Pas
Un Mari Qui Lance Sa Femme

At the Porte Saint-Martin

1865 La Biche au Bois
Les Femmes Savantes

At the Odéon

1866 Le Jeu de l'Amour et du Hasard

1867 Les Femmes Savantes
Le Roi Lear
Le Legs
Athalie
Le Testament de Césare Girodot

François le Champi
Le Marquis de Villemer
Le Drame de la Rue de la Paix
La Gloire de Molière

1868 Kean
La Lotérie de Mariage

1869 Le Passant
Le Bâtarde

1870 L'Affranchi
L'Autre

1871 Jean Marie
Mademoiselle Aisse
Ruy Blas

At the Comédie Française

1872 Mlle. de Belle Isle
Le Cid
Britannicus

1873 Le Mariage de Figaro
Dalila
L'Absent
Chez l'Avocat
Andromache
Phèdre

1874 Le Sphinx
L'Absent
Chez l'Avocat

152

La Belle Paule
Zaïre
Phèdre

1875 La Fille de Roland
Gabrielle

1876 L'Etrangère
La Nuit de Mai
Rome Vaincue

1877 Hernani

1878 Othello
Amphitryon

1879 Mithridate

1880 L'Aventurière
Les Enfants d'Édouard
Le Sphinx
Adrienne Lecouvreur
Froufrou
La Dame aux Camélias
Phèdre (recording)

1881 La Princèsse Georges

1882 Fédora

1883 Nana Sahib

1884 Macbeth
Théodora

1885 Marion Delormé

1886 Hamlet
Le Maître des Forges
L'Aveu

Touring the World

1887 La Tosca

1888 Françillon

1889 Léna

1890 Jeanne d'Arc
Cléopâtre
Pauline Blanchard
La Dame de Chalant

1891 Gringoire

At the Théâtre de la Renaissance

1893 Les Rois

1894 Izéil
La Femme de Claude
Gismonda

1895 Magda
La Princèsse Lointaine

1896 Lorenzaccio
Izeyl (recording)

1897 Spiritisme
La Samaritaine
Les Mauvais Bergers

1898 La Ville Morte
Lysiane
Médée

At the Théatre Sarah Bernhardt

1899 Hamlet

1900 L'Aiglon
Cyrano de Bèrgèrac
Le Duel d'Hamlet (film)

1901 La Pluie et le Beau Temps
Les Précieuses Ridicules

1902 Francesca da Rimini
Sapho
Théroigne de Méricourt
La Fiancée du Timbalier (recording)
Lucie (recording)
La Chanson d'Eviradnus (recording)

1903 Andromache
Werther
Le Légende du Coeur
Plus que Reine
Jeanne Wedekind
La Sorcière
Le Lac (recording)
La Samaritaine (recording)
Les Vieux (recording)
Un Evangile (recording)

1903 Phèdre (recording)
La Mort d'Izail (recording)
Théroigne de Méricourt (recording)
Un Peu de Musique (recording)
Le Légende de Siècles (recording)

1904 Le Festin de la Mort
Bohemos
Varennes

1905 Angelo
Esther
Pelléas et Mélisande
Adrienne Lecouvreur

1906 La Vierge d'Avila

1907 Les Bouffons
Le Vert-Galant
La Belle au Bois Dormant

1908 La Courtisane de Corinthe

Cléonice
La Tosca (film)
Les Bouffons (recording)

1909 La Nuit de Mai
La Fille de Rabenstein
Le Procès de Jeanne d'Arc

1910 La Beffa
Le Bois Sacre
Madame X
Judas
L'Aiglon: Torch! (recording)
Phèdre (recording)
La Samaritaine (recording)

1911 Lucrèce Borgia
La Dame aux Camélias (film aka
Camille)

1912 Une Nuit de Noël sous Le Terreur
Adrienne Lecouvreur (film)
Sarah Bernhardt à Belle Isle
(documentary film)
Les Amours de la Reine Elisabeth (film)

1913 Jeanne Doré

1914 Tout à Coup

1915 Les Cathédrales
Ceux de Chez Nous (documentary film)

1916 La Mort de Cléopâtre
L'Holocauste
Du Théâtre au Champ d'Honneur
Vitrail
Hécube
Le Faux Modèle
Le Marchand de Venise
L'Etoile dans la Nuit
Jeanne Doré (film)

1918 Les Mères Françaises (film)
L'Etoile dans la Nuit (recording)
La Prière pour Nos Ennemis (recording)

1919 It Happened in Paris (film)

1920 Athalie
Daniel
Comment on Écrit l'Histoire

1921 La Gloire
Daniel (film)

1922 Régine Arnaud

1923 La Voyante (film)

Bibliography

Arvidson, Linda. *When the Movies Were Young.* New York: Dover Publications, 1969.

Auster, Albert. *Actresses and Suffragists.* New York: Drama Book Publishers, 1983.

Barring, Maurice. *Sarah Bernhardt.* New York: D. Appleton-Century, Inc., 1934.

Bell, W. Bruce. *Show: The Man Who Outwitted Sarah Bernhardt.* October, 1964.

Bernhardt, Lysiane. *Sarah Bernhardt Ma Grand mére.* Paris: Editions du Pavois, 1947.

Bernhardt, Sarah. *Memories of My Life.* New York: D. Appleton, 1907.

Blaisdell, G. F. *Moving Picture World: Bernhardt in La Tosca.* New York: Chalmers, October, 1912.

Brazier, M. H. *Stage and Screen.* Boston: The Plimpton Press, 1920.

Brownlow, Kevin. *Hollywood: The Pioneers.* New York: Alfred A. Knopf, 1980.

Bush, W. Stephen. *Moving Picture World: Queen Elizabeth.* New York: Chalmers, August, 1912.

_____. *Moving Picture World: Bernhardt and Rejane in Pictures.* New York: Chalmers, March, 1912.

Carr, Daphne. *Pictureplay: The Last Role of Sarah Bernhardt.* New York: Street and Smith, November 1923.

Caward, Neil G. *Motography: Sarah Bernhardt at Home Review.* Chicago: 1915.

Exhibitors Trade Review. November 22, 1919.

Feinstein, Robert. *In the Groove: Sarah Bernhardt and the Bettini Recording Legacy.* Michigan: Antique Phonograph Society, 2002.

Ford, Charles. *Films in Review: Notes on a Dying Legend.* Lancaster, Pennsylvania: National Board of Review of Motion Pictures, Inc., December, 1954, vol. 5, no. 10.

Fulton, A. R. *Motion Pictures: The Development of an Art.* Norman: University of Oklahoma Press, 1980.

Giebler, A. H. *Moving Picture World: No Operation for Bernhardt.* New York: Chalmers, November, 1918.

Glass, Gaston. *Movie Magazine: Sarah Bernhardt, a Memory.* New York: Movie Weekly Publishing Corp., January, 1926.

Grau, Robert. *Picture Play Magazine: The Sarah Bernhardt of Today.* New York: Street and Street Corporation, December, 1915.

Harding, Colin, and Simon Popple. *In the Kingdom of Shadows: A Companion to the Early Cinema.* Teaneck, N.H.: Fairleigh Dickinson University Press, 1996.

Hillard-Hughes, Albert. *Sarah Bernhardt on the Screen.* New York: Film Fan Monthly, 1969.

_____. *The Silent Picture: Bernhardt on the Screen.* Summer, 1970.

Koszarski, Richard. *An Evening's Entertainment.* Berkeley: The University of Cambridge Press, 1990.

Le Cinéma. Washington: The Motion Picture Guild, September, 1927.

Le Théâtre et Comédie Illustré: Sarah Bernhardt. June, 1923.

Leyda, Jay, and Charles Mussur. *Before Hollywood.* New York: Hudson Hills Press, 1987.

Macgowan, Kenneth. *Behind the Screen.* New York: Delacorte Press, 1965.

Mamoulian, Rouben. *Theatre Arts: Bernhardt vs Duse.* September, 1957.

Motion Picture Review. New York: Brewster, November 22, 1919.

Moving Picture World: Adrienne Lecouvreur. New York: Chalmers, February, 1913.

Moving Picture World: Bernhardt and Rejane. New York: Chalmers, February, 1912.

Moving Picture World: Bernhardt Conquers New World. New York: Chalmers, March, 1912.

Moving Picture World: Bernhardt Exclusively with Société Film D'Art. New York: Chalmers, March, 1912.

Moving Picture World: Bernhardt Invited to Be Guest of Honor at Anniversary Celebration of First Feature. New York: Chalmers, February, 1922.

Moving Picture World: Bernhardt Now Partly American. New York: Chalmers, December, 1915.

Moving Picture World: Bernhardt's Last Year on the Screen. New York: Chalmers, October, 1915.

Moving Picture World: Éclair Presents Mme. Bernhardt in Pictures. New York: Chalmers, November, 1911.

Moving Picture World: It Happened in Paris. New York: Chalmers, January, 1920.

Moving Picture World: Murray to Manage Bernhardt. New York: Chalmers, October,1916.

Moving Picture World: Rights to Mothers of France Unsold. New York: Chalmers, February, 1917.

Moving Picture World: Sarah Bernhardt at Home. New York: Chalmers, July, 1915.

Moving Picture World: Sarah Bernhardt Pleased with Pictures. New York: Chalmers, September, 1912.

New York Times Encyclopedia of Film. New York: Times Books, 1984.

Noble, Iris. *Great Lady of the Theater.* New York: Julian Messner, Inc. 1960.

Pratt, George. *Spellbound in Darkness.* Greenwich: University of Rochester, 1966.

Ramsaye, Terry. *A Million and One Nights.* New York: Simon and Schuster, 1926.

Réné, Jeanne, and Charles Ford. *Histoire Encyclopédique du Cinéma.* Paris, 1947.

Robins, Elizabeth. *North American Review: On Seeing Madame Bernhardt's Hamlet.* December, 1900.

Row, Arthur William. *Sarah the Divine.* New York: Comet Press Books, 1951.

Rueff, Suze. *I Knew Sarah Bernhardt.* London: Frederick Muller Ltd., 1982.

Skinner, Cornelia Otis. *Madame Sarah.* Boston: The Riverside Press Cambridge, 1966.

Stokes, John, Michael Booth, and Susan Bassnett. *The Actress in Her Time.* Cambridge: Cambridge University Press, 1988.

Tellegen, Lou. *Women Have Been Kind.* New York: Vanguard Press, 1931.

Van Loan, H. H. *Motion Picture Magazine: The Divine Sarah.* January, 1916.

Variety. New York, New York: Garland, 1983.

Wagenknecht, Edward. *Seven Daughters of the Theater.* Norman: University of Oklahoma Press, 1964.

Wid's Daily: Review. March 7, 1920.

Woon, Basil. *The Real Sarah Bernhardt.* New York: Boni and Liveright, 1924.

Index

Abrams, Leon 147
L'Absent 19
An Actress's Romance 117
Adriana Lecouvreur (opera) 117
Adrienne Lecouvreur 22, 24, 89, 94, 117–119
Agnel, Raymond 146
L'Aiglon 26, 27, 46, 91, 121
L'Aiglon (recording) 48, 71
Aine, Coquelin 90, 91
Alixe 24
Les Amours de la Reine Elisabeth 89, 109
Andromaque 19, 26
Angelo, Jean 9
Les Annales du théâtre et de la musique 91
Antoine, André 31
Atlantide 9
Au Champs d'Honneur 37
Auber, M. 14
Aunt Rosine 13
Auxetophone 91
L'Aventurière 20

Baring, Maurice 38, 40
Barnum, P.T. 35
Baron, Michel 117
Bartet, Julia 118
Baur, Harry 95, 146, 149
The Beatles 7
Beck, Martin 10, 37
Bell, Chichester A. 41
Belle Isle 26
Bernard, Raymond 94, 121, 124, 130
Bernard, Tristan 94, 121, 124
Bernhardt, Maurice 16, 31, 36, 47, 48, 52, 62, 63, 107, 150
Bernhardt, Sarah: acting debut 15; Bettini recordings 44;

birth 13; at the Comédie Française 18; death 38, 150; destroying *La Tosca* film 92; 1880 American tour 23; 1891 world tour 25; Farewell Tour 27; filming *Adrienne Lecouvreur* 94; filming *Camille* 92; filming *Jeanne Doré* 94; filming *Mères Française* 95; filming *Queen Elizabeth* 93; final American Tour 37; first audition 14; first recording session 43; at the Gymnase 16; *Hamlet* play and film 89; meeting Lou Tellegen 28; 1905-6 leg amputation 35; at the Odeon 16–17; play and film of *La Voyante* 95; at the Théâtre de la Renaissance 25; in Vaudeville 36
Berton, Mme. Pierre 147, 149
Bettini, Lieutenant Gianni 43, 44
Bettini Micro-Phonograph 45
Bettini Recording Laboratory 40, 47
Between Friends 35
The Birth of the Talkies 91
Bisson 10
Blaisdelle, G.F. 99
Blue Amberol Records 41
Les Bouffons (recording) 47, 48, 67, 71
The Breeze Tells (recording) 67
Brindeau, Jeanne 146
Britannicus 14
Brockliss, Frank 92
Brunton Studios 138
Bush, W. Stephen 106, 114
Butt, W. Lawson 138

Cain, Henri 49, 83
Calmettes, Albert 92, 97, 98, 100
Camille 23, 36, 46, 47, 92, 100, 101, 102, 103, 105, 106, 109, 111; film score 105–106
Campbell, Mrs. Patrick 27
Candlelight Club 9
Capellani, Paul 100
Carr, Daphne 148
Casanova, Eva 35
Castle de Hulst 29
Cathédrale de Westminister 38
Les Cathédrales 35, 38
Caward, Neil G. 107
Ceux de Chez Nous 89
Chameroy, M. 109
La Chanson d'Eviradnus (recording) 48
Chaplin, Charlie 7
Chenu, Mme. Marguerite 90, 97
Chez l'Avocat 19
A Christmas Night Under the Terror 36
chronophone system 91
Cilea, Francesco 117
Cinématographes Éclaire 97
The Clairvoyant 95
Clark, John R. 127, 128, 130
Cléopâtre 21, 45, 98
Cocteau, Jean 101
Comédie Française 14, 15, 16, 18, 20, 105, 117, 149
Comment On Ecrit l'Histoire 38
Connor, William F. 92, 117, 121, 125
Conservatoire 13, 14, 15, 31
Coppée, François 18, 58
Costa, Mlle. 121

Cunningham, Jack 138
Cyrano de Bergerac 26, 90, 108

Dalila 19
La Dame aux Camélias 8, 22, 23, 25, 26, 89, 100–104
Damita, Lili 95, 146, 149
Daniel 38, 89, 140, 143, 144, 145, 146
The Death of Izail (recording) 62
De Brabender, Mlle 13
Decoeur, M. 109
De Max, Edouard 97, 100
Le Démon du Jeu 16
De Morny, Duc 13
De Musset, Alfred 47, 51
Deneubourg, M. 100
De Saxe, Maurice 117
Desfontaines, Henri 100, 109, 117
Dickson, W. K. L. 7
Dione, Rose 138
Divorces 98
Don Giovanni 90
Dorval, Marie-Louise 109
Du Théâtre au Champ d'Honneur 85
Le Duel d'Hamlet 89, 96, 97
Dumas fils, Alexandre 100, 106
Dunn, Winifred 138

Éclair American Company 92, 100
Edison, Thomas 7, 24, 41, 42, 43, 47, 71, 75, 79
Edison Amberol Cylinder 49
Edison Company 89
Edison Diamond Discs 41
Edison wax cylinders 97
Embolden, William M. 107
Engadine Corporation 92, 113
Engel, Joseph 92, 113
Esther 26
Eternal Springtime 32
L'Etoile dans la Nuit (recording) 47, 49, 83
L'Etrangère 20, 22
Un Evangel (A Gospel) (recording) 48, 58
The Exploits of Elaine 95
The Explorer 35

Fairbanks, Douglas 115
Fall of Troy 92
Falstaff 90
Famous Players Film Company 92, 93, 94, 109, 113, 115

Farewell American Tours 27, 37
Farrar, Geraldine 31, 35, 136
Fédora 98
Feinstein, Robert 43, 43
Les Femmes Savantes 15
Feyder, Jacques
La Fiancée du Timbalier (recording) 47, 50
Film d'Art 92, 97, 99, 100, 105, 111, 117, 121
Films in Review 7
The Flame of the Desert 35
Ford, Charles 7, 117
The Fortune Teller 146, 147, 148, 149, 150
Fratellini, François 146
Frederick, Pauline 35, 115
French-American Film Company 100, 109, 111
Frohman, Daniel 93, 113
Frou Frou 44
Fuller, Loie 31

Gance, Abel 114
Gaumont, Leon 90
Gaumont Company 91
Gaumont Phono-Scenes 91
Geduld, Harry M. 91
Gibory, Alphonse 146
Gismonda 25
Glass, Gaston 45
La Gloirie 38
Goldwyn, Samuel 35
A Gospel (recording) 58
Grau, Robert 126
Guerinon, Emile 49. 94
Guitry, Lucien 97
Guitry, Sacha 146, 147
Gunn, Charles 138

Hamlet 26, 27, 91, 92, 96, 97
Hammond, Percy 36
Hard, Judith Van 14
Hart, William S. 115
Hartford, David 138, 139
Hearst Greek Theater 27
Hernani 20, 22
Hervieu, Paul Ernest 48, 63
Hervil, Rene 121, 130
Hugo, Victor 10, 18, 43, 47, 48, 50, 66

Iphigénie 15
It Happened in Paris 89, 138, 139

Izeyl (recording) 47
Iziel 43, 63

Jalabert, Berthe 130
Jarret, Mr. Edward 20, 21, 24
Jeanne, Réné 117
Jeanne Doré 35, 89, 94, 121–128; film score 129
Jeanne the Maid of Orleans 46
Le Jeu de l'Amour et du Hasard 18
Joad 18
Jolie Susie 8
Jourjon, Charles 92
Junie de Britannicus 19

Keline Optical Company 96
kinetophones 89
kinetoscope 89

Le Lac (recording) 47, 52
Laemmle, Carl 128
The Lake (recording) 47
Langlois, Henri 107
Langrange, Louise 130
Larson, Victoria Tietze 13
Lasky Film Company 35
Laurent, Jeanne-Marie 95
Lavedam, Henri 91
Leah 16
Lecouvreur, Adrienne (actress) 117
Le Légende des Siècles XV (recording) 48
Legouve, Ernest 117
Let Not Man Put Asunder 35
Ligne, Henri 16
Lincoln, Abraham 23, 24
Lincoln, Mary Todd 24
Lioret, Henri 90
Lorenzaccio 25
Louis XV 117
Lou-Tellegen 8, 28, 31, 33, 34, 35, 49, 93, 100, 101, 102, 104, 109, 112, 113, 114, 116, 117, 118
Lucie (recording) 47, 51
Lucrezia Borgia 36
Lyceum Theater 8, 113
Lyses, Charlotte

Mack, Hayward 138
Madame Sans-Gêne 92, 99, 100
Madame X 122
Mademoiselle de Belle Isle 18
Maeterlinck, Louis 27
Magda 27

Magnier, Pierre 96
La Maison sans Enfants 16
Mamoulian, Rouben 140, 142, 143
Le Mariage de Figaro 19
Marquet, Mary 95, 146, 149
Matzene, M. 138
Maurel, Victor 90
Maurice, Clement 96
Maury, M. 100
Maxcy, W.G. 9
Maxudian, M. 109
Meighan, Thomas 115
Melchoir, George 146, 149
Menlo Park 24, 42, 47
Mercanton, Louis 13, 38, 92, 109, 117, 121, 132, 133, 135, 146, 147
Mères Française 36, 89, 95, 130, 131, 132, 133, 134, 135, 136, 137, 137; poster 131
Metropolitan Museum of Art 32
Meydieu, M. 13
Meyer, Frank 92
Michelangelo
A Million and One Nights 113
Minter, Mary Miles 115
Molière 15
Morand, Eugène 26, 35, 47,
Moreau, Emile 92, 96, 109
Morris, Clara 24
La Mort d'Izail (recording) 48, 62
Mothers of France 95, 130, 131, 132, 133, 134, 135, 136, 137, 138
Motography 94
Mounet, Paul 31, 97
Mounet-Sully 92, 99
Mozart 90
My Double Life: The Memoirs of Sarah Bernhardt 13
The Mysteries of New York 95

Nadar, Felix 15, 25
Napoléon 114
Nathalie, Madame 15
Nauck, Kurt 46
Nazimova, Alla 35
Nilsson, Anna Q. 35
La Nuit de Mai 9

Oedipus Rex 92, 99
The Old (recording) 56
L'Opinion Nationale 15

Paquerette, Mme. 146
Paramount Films 114
Paris Exposition Universelle de 1900 89, 97
Le Passant 16, 18
Pathé Co. 47, 51
"Pathe Gazette" 38, 143
Pathé News 141
Patrie 98
Payen, Louis 49
Pearl of the Army 95
Pelléas and Mélisande 27
Père Lachaise Cemetery 40, 150
The Perils of Pauline 95
Un Peu de Musique (recording) 43, 48, 66
Phèdre (play) 19, 20, 22, 24, 26, 27, 42, 43, 61, 76
Phèdre (recording) 47, 48, 49, 60, 75
Phono-Cinema Theatre 90, 96
Piaf, Edith 46
Pickford, Mary 7, 115
Pitou 100
Porter, Edwin 113
Pouctal, Henri 100
A Prayer for Our Enemies (recording) 85
Les Précieuses Ridiculous 90
Presley, Elvis 7
Prière Pour Nos Ennemis (recording) 37, 44, 49, 84, 85
La Princesse George 22
Puccini 98
The Puppet 35

Queen Elizabeth 7, 28, 34, 35, 38, 92, 93, 94, 109, 111, 112, 113, 115, 116, 121
Queen Wilhelmina 29

Rachel 14
Racine, Jean 10, 14, 20, 48, 49
The Redeeming Sin 35
Reggers, Madame 38
Régine Arman 38
Reid, Wallace 115
Réjane, Gabrielle Charlotte 90, 92, 99
Renoir, August
Le Rêve de Théroigne de Méricourt (recording) 63
Richepin, Jean 130, 132, 134, 135, 136

Robert, Henry
Robins, Elizabeth 96
Rockefeller 9
Rockwell, Helen 138, 139
Rodin, Auguste 30, 31
Les Rois 25
Romane, Mlle. 109, 114
Rome Vaincue 20
Rostand, Edmond 10, 26, 48, 55, 91, 108
Rostand, Mme. Edmond 48, 46, 91
Ruy Blas 18, 20

Salomé 31
La Samaritaine (play) 46; (recording) 48, 49, 54, 55, 79
Sarah Bernhardt à Belle-Isle 26, 89, 107, 108, 109
Sarah Bernhardt Artist and Icon 107
Sarah Bernhardt at Home 26, 89, 107, 108, 109
"Sarah Bernhardt Special" 25
Sarcey, Francisque 19
Sardou, Victorien 10, 23, 26, 36, 97, 98, 99
Schwob, Marcel 26, 96
Scribe, Eugène 117
Seylor, Suzanne 100, 121
Shakespeare, William 26, 96
Signoret, Gabriel 130
Silvestre, Paul-Armand 47
Simsolo, Noel
Sinatra, Frank 7
Sinn, Clarene E. 105
Skinner, Cornelia Otis 147
Société Film d'Art 99, 105
Société Française des Films and Cinématographs Éclair 92, 97
Soman, Sheila 46, 50, 51, 54, 60, 66, 71, 75, 79
The Song of Eviradnus 48
La Sorcière 26
Le Sphinx 22
The Star in the Night (recording) 49, 83
Stella Dallas 122
Stewart, Anita 115
Stoullig, Edmond 91
Un Sujet de Roman 38, 147
Swanson, Gloria 115

Tainter, Charles Sumner 41
Talmadge, Norma 115
Tanguay, Eva 36

Théâtre de la Renaissance 25
Théâtre de L'Odeon 18, 20, 31
Théâtre du Gymnase 16
Théâtre Sarah Bernhardt 25, 26, 39
Théodora 23, 24, 33
Théroigne de Méricourt (recording) 48, 63, 65
Three Bernard Brothers 30
tinfoil recording 42
Titanic 112
La Tosca 25, 26, 28, 89, 91, 92, 97, 98, 99, 100, 101
Tout à Coup 38
Twain, Mark 6
The Two Pigeons 14, 15, 24
Tyrad Pictures Inc. 138
Universal 126

Universal Film Company 92, 121, 125, 126, 128

Valentino, Rudolph 7
Valérie 15
Van Loan, H. H. 123
Vaudeville 35, 37
Verdi 90
Verneuil, Louis 140
Les Vieux (The Old Men) (recording) 48, 56
Vitagraph 35
La Voyante 38, 89, 95, 146–150

Waal, Peter van 5, 9, 16, 23, 40, 42, 43, 55, 65, 131
wax cylinder photographs 42, 43

Webel, Professor Alissa 46, 52, 56, 58, 62, 63, 67, 83, 85
Western Film Exchange 92
White, Pearl 95
Wilson, Woodrow 112
The Woman and the Puppet 31
Women Have Been Kind 29
Woon, Basil 147
The World and Its Woman 35
World Films 130

Yorska, Madame 138, 139, 40

Zaharof, Sir Basil 107
Zaïre 19
Zamaçois, Miquel 48, 67
Zonophone Company 48
Zukor, Adolph 8, 92, 93, 94, 113, 115